Also by Gail Saltz, M.D.

Becoming Real: Defeating the Stories We Tell Ourselves That Hold Us Back

Gail Saltz, M.D.

2/22

Praise for *Anatomy of a Secret Life*

"In this gripping book, Gail Saltz analyzes the origins and consequences of hidden lives, articulating both the seductions that secrets hold and the terrible danger they pose as they undermine the capacity for intimacy. This is a brave examination of the balance between safety and loneliness that we all negotiate at one level or another."

—Andrew Solomon, author of *The Noonday Demon: An Atlas of Depression*

"Saltz writes with eloquence and sophistication . . . In titillating anecdotes, Saltz describes killers, addicts, and cheaters . . . Should you find yourself skipping ahead to the next juicy anecdote, that'll be your little secret."

—*New York Times Book Review*

"Saltz takes us on an engrossing and voyeuristic journey through the secret lives of several people, some composites from her psychoanalytic practice . . . While most people's secrets aren't as dramatic as the stories related here, this book serves as a cautionary tale of how a secret is formed, lived, justified—and eventually exposed."

—*Publishers Weekly*

"In her fascinating new book, Dr. Gail Saltz explores the impulse to create and nurture alter egos . . . *Anatomy of a Secret Life* is based on the latest research and is the definitive work on how secret lives are formed, lived, justified, and exposed. Dr. Saltz's psychoanalytic study of this engrossing and potentially dangerous phenomenon can help us all to better understand the intricacies of being human."

—Kind Features Syndicate, Inc.

[ANATOMY OF A SECRET LIFE]

○ ● ○ ● ○ ● ○ ● ○ ● ○ ● ○ ● ○ ●

Are the People in Your Life Hiding Something You Should Know?

Morgan Road Books
New York

A hardcover edition of this book was originally published in 2006
by Morgan Road Books.

Published in the United States by Morgan Road Books, an imprint of
The Doubleday Broadway Publishing Group, a division of Random House, Inc.,
New York.
www.morganroadbooks.com

Book design by Michael Collica

ISBN 978-0-7679-2304-0

PRINTED IN THE UNITED STATES OF AMERICA

10 9 8 7 6 5 4 3 2 1

First Paperback Edition

[Author's Note]

Over the last thirteen years I have seen many patients in practice in addition to interacting with people via my work in the media. I have drawn on their stories in order to illustrate the experiences I describe in this book. Their stories are composites, and I have invented all the names and identifying data used in the stories. Any resulting resemblance to persons living or dead is entirely coincidental and unintentional.

To Lenny, with whom I share my secrets and love

It is a joy to be hidden, but a disaster not to be found.

—D. W. Winnicott

[Contents]

[Acknowledgments]

Thank you to my husband, Len, and to my daughters, Emily, Kimberly, and Tori, who are my inspiration, my touchstone, my greatest joy. Lenny, without your support, encouragement, and pride in what I do it would not be possible for me to do it at all. You amaze me every day with your strength, your patience, your empathy, and your ability to give us so much love. Thank you to our amazing daughters, who are so smart, so fun, and so caring. Special thanks for tolerating times when I was at work on this book. I am one lucky mom!

A special thank-you to Marly Rusoff, who never ceases to amaze me with her energy, creativity, warmth, humor, and ability to spot just what's needed. You made this a better book. Thank you to Sandi Mendelson, who has continued to support me with her smart and savvy guidance.

I would like to thank my editor, Amy Hertz, for her vision, her wonderful critiques and additions, which made this a much better book. Thank you as well to Marc Haeringer for his thoughtful insights and careful attention, which also greatly improved this book. Thanks to Nate Brown for his efficient handling of all matters in such a kind and polite manner. Big thanks to all the staff at Doubleday Broadway and Morgan Road Books for their great enthusiasm and support of this project.

Last, but perhaps most important, thank you to all the patients and people who have reached out to me in my office, and via e-mail, letter, or phone call, to share their secrets with me in the hopes of understanding the secrets they keep from themselves. Thank you for trusting me to be your guide on the road to self-understanding.

[ANATOMY OF A SECRET LIFE]

[1 • THE SECRET LIFE]

> Who knows what evil lurks in the hearts of men?
>
> —from *The Shadow* (1930–54)

A woman in the doctor's waiting room natters on about the weather, oblivious to the fact that no one's really listening. Maybe she's a chatterbox. Or maybe she's terminally ill.

A man stands in line at the bank, frowning to himself. Maybe he's overdrawn. Or maybe when he gets home he'll tell his wife he no longer loves her.

A child on the swing in the playground wears long sleeves, though it's the height of summer. Maybe her mother is overprotective. Or maybe her mother beats her black-and-blue.

The husband in bed turns to face you. He may be thinking only of you. Or he may be thinking only of your closest friend.

The man on the treadmill next to yours at the gym runs as fast as he can, turning his iPod's volume up as high as it will go. Maybe he can't lose those last five pounds. Or maybe he can't get rid of the image of that woman he met at the bar, and can't drown out her screams.

And you: Maybe you know yourself. Or maybe you don't.

We all have secrets; we live and breathe them every day. We may not know what one another's secrets are, but we know they're there. They're *always* there, invisible presences in everyone's lives, the subtext beneath the text, the almost uttered but then swallowed sentence, the cryptic, fleeting expression on someone's face. Humankind's basic needs are food, water, and shelter, but secrets aren't too far down the list of essentials. They provide a safe haven that allows us the freedom to explore who we are, to establish an identity that is uniquely our own. But even the deepest secrets can also be shared; they are the currency of close relationships, the coin of exclusivity, sometimes the key to love itself.

Under some circumstances, however, secrets can also be profound sources of shame, guilt, anxiety, despair. While we're always surprised when we learn about the misbehavior or strange habits and predilections of friends or public figures, in another way we aren't surprised at all. We've grown to expect that such behavior will crop up occasionally, that unusual personality traits will be routinely revealed.

And we expect it not only because we've seen it in other friends or public figures (and we certainly have), but because *we* have been known to behave in this manner sometimes, too, and because we also possess well-concealed traits and habits and interests that would be considered strange by other people.

Secrets can cause people to behave in ways that seem entirely out of character—to go to any desperate length to conceal what simply *must* be hidden, at all costs. They can require so much vigilance and attentiveness and sheer time that they begin to dominate an entire life, in effect *becoming* that person's life. Everything that is unrelated to the secret becomes secondary and irrelevant and is cast off. A kind of fear—sometimes, nearly a paranoia—sets in at the mere idea of the secret being unearthed. *What if someone finds out I stole that money? What if my employer reads my blog and sees that I'm not just an ordinary nanny, but that I also have an active sex life and have taken Xstasy? What if my best friend finds out I hate her husband? What if my most private self is revealed? Then everything will be lost.* The possibility of discovery is played out again and again like a sickening loop of film.

Many secret lives remain sub-rosa for surprisingly long periods of time. Relationships are kept hidden through sheer ingenuity, and dark acts stay in perpetual darkness. The serial killer learns to live with secrecy as his constant companion; so does the illicit lover, or the tax cheat, or the thief. The balance of power between secret and secret-keeper is constantly being negotiated. If we can control our own secrets, making sure they occupy the place we want them to, then our lives can seem manageable. But when our secrets start to control *us*—and far too often they do—then a normal life clicks over into something else: a secret life.

When that happens, everything changes. Suddenly we find ourselves forced to give up any remaining vestiges of openness and casualness and instead submit full-time to the exacting rules that the secret life inevitably demands.

And the reason we are forced to submit in this way is that the secrets we keep to ourselves are only half the story. The other half is composed of the secrets we keep *from* ourselves. These are the ones that have been forced underground over time, in some instances since early childhood. They are the ones that we simply don't want to know about, so embarrassed or enraged would we feel if we were forced to confront them head-on. Glimmers of those feelings occasionally surface without our understanding why; we may overreact to seemingly trivial events, or have a strong response to a particular person, or be disturbed by a dream we've dreamed without really knowing why. In these moments, we've somehow entered the cordoned-off territory of the secret from the self, and while we may not understand this has happened, we know enough to tighten up security even further.

But without access to these inner secrets, we can't really know ourselves at all. Instead, we're forced to spend our lives in a state of continual vagueness, ignorant of the reasons behind our own actions and perceptions.

In the following chapters I take the basic concept of secrecy—which is intrinsic to everyone, though sometimes subtly so—and magnify it so it can be viewed as the powerful, dramatic, life-shaping force it is. Some of the stories trace the ways that people's lives have been destroyed because of the secrets they keep. Other stories tell of lives that have flourished because of the layers of complexity and richness that secrecy provides them. At times, secret-keeping proves to be a question of choice, or even luxury; at other times, it has life-or-death consequences.

A few of the secret-keepers here are composites of people I have seen in my practice as a psychoanalyst. Their circumstances might seem extraordinary at times, but they arise out of the ordinary complications of daily life. I've chosen them precisely because they are representative. You might even recognize aspects of yourself.

Other stories in this book come right from history: a world-famous hero who, at the height of his fame, secretly fathered many children with several women; a composer of international renown whose sexual predilections might have forced him to commit suicide; a beloved military figure who could find sexual pleasure only at the receiving end of a whip. If these descriptions sound far removed from your own life, that's deliberate on my part; some of these lives have been chosen for their sweeping, dramatic scale, which makes it easier to see not just the ways in which specific secret-keepers operate, but the ways in which *all* secret-keepers do. And that includes every one of us.

"Know thyself," urged Socrates, while a more modern maxim insists, "Ignorance is bliss." The two proverbs, often quoted, deliver opposing messages. Some people live by one, some by the other. But most people, at different times in their lives and in various ways, live by both. They try to remain open and honest as much as possible, keeping some details fuzzy and vague and hidden from certain people, while concealing other details from everyone, including themselves.

Secrets: Can't live with them, can't live without them. They are here with us at all times, swirling around us, causing problems, generating excitement, forcing us to be watchful. "I know something you don't know," goes the singsong of children. This is true for all of us. We *all* know things that other people don't, things we'd love to blurt out but that we simply can't. Secrets are like a long inhaled breath that can't wait to be exhaled, and perhaps never will. They are maddening, thrilling, dangerous. Secrets routinely meet in the air and then disperse, unspoken. And every day, secret-keepers keep on doing what they do: living one life, and then living another.

[2 • THE SECRET LIFE OF THE MIND]

I'm Chevy Chase, and you're not.

—from *Saturday Night Live* (c. 1975)

It was loneliness that drew her to the desktop computer at first, and later on it was excitement. Adrian always made sure to finish her homework first, and then she kissed her mother good night (her father was usually traveling) and went upstairs to her bedroom, where she would sit in front of the pale blue glowing monitor, living an IM life that was so much more compelling and fulfilling than the one she really lived.

Her early years had been easy and pleasurable, surrounded by friends. But starting in sixth grade, the line between cool and uncool began to thicken, and Adrian found herself falling on the wrong side of the divide. She didn't mind. She could always hang out with the other girls in this group and pretend that none of them cared about being uncool. But for the alpha girls, coolness evolved into cruelty. No matter how Adrian dressed, or what she said or did, the alpha girls beat her down with their nasty words, mocking her clumsy attempts to fit in. They'd taken a page right out of the movie *Mean Girls*, and though Adrian tried to believe, as she wrote in her diary, that they were just using her as a scapegoat and that she shouldn't take it personally, she took the mean girls' words to heart. She was ugly, she wrote in that diary, and fat, and stupid, and a complete loser. She might as well die right now. Even Stephen King's Carrie had it better than she did. So Adrian, a girl with deep-set, hungry eyes and an awkward way of carrying herself as she navigated the treacherous corridors of school, retreated into herself.

The Internet helped her do that, providing an alternate corridor that she could walk down easily, and where no one would hiss cruel names at her, or casually stick out a foot so that she would stumble and fall. Adrian began IMing every night, and while in her daily life she was an outcast, here she was popular. Different anonymous people chatted with her, both male and female, and she found herself writing responses in the shorthand that such interactions required. The rhythms of the chats were friendly and funny and sometimes flirtatious. She took the screen name Exotica, a name that had just popped into her head out of nowhere, which was funny to her, because

Adrian, at fifteen, with her slightly lumpy nose and scattering of acne and clumsy demeanor, was the furthest thing in the world from exotic. But no one online had to know that.

One night she began talking with a guy who called himself chai83. He lived in the suburbs of New Jersey, only an hour and a half from her own Long Island suburb. "Hey, Exotica," he wrote. "How u doin?" To which Adrian replied, "Exotica is bored 2nite. Tell me something interesting." The tone of her words was playful and teasing; she'd never spoken like this to anyone before. But as "Exotica" chatted on through the evening and into the night, long after her mother had gone to bed, she started to open up to chai83. She kept a balance between her actual, Adrian self and her new, Exotica persona, mixing true details (chestnut hair, dark brown eyes) with made-up ones (age eighteen, worked as a bartender at a trendy club in Manhattan).

Though her own details were a stew of the real and the false, she never questioned whether chai83's own story was entirely true. He said that he was twenty-two, with black wavy hair and dark blue eyes, and that he was an aspiring actor who made his living as a waiter. Back and forth, they traded anecdotes and aspirations, mostly using suggestive language. This went on and on for a matter of weeks. Adrian seemed less troubled by the mean girls at school, and their catty comments simply floated past her. She was moving further away from school itself. She stopped listening in class, and began failing tests. It got to the point where Adrian skipped doing her homework altogether and just went straight to the computer, where chai83 was inevitably waiting. For an actor who had a day job and was often going off on auditions, he was online a surprising amount of time.

Then one night, chai83 said he wanted to "take my friendship with u to a new level." He asked Exotica to meet him in the parking lot of the mall in his hometown. Tentatively, she agreed. "How will I know u, Exotica?" he asked. "I will be the exotic one," she told him.

Three days later, after Adrian's body had been found in a swamp in central New Jersey, her desperate mother wept to the policemen who came to her home that her daughter was a studious girl who would never go anywhere unsafe or do anything stupid. And when the sergeant asked if Adrian had kept secrets from her, her mother shook her head no with conviction.

To have secrets is to be human. To find in a private world a personal identity is an essential part of what it means to be a member of our species. The ability to have a secret is the thing that gives birth to our sense of ourselves in early childhood, and the secrets we keep and share are what shape our relationships for the rest of our lives. Here, then, is a crash course in developmental psychology, as it relates to the complex and very human art of secrecy.

Once, none of us had any secrets. Our life in the climate-controlled aquarium of the womb was all mom, all the time. We were one with this woman whom we hadn't even met. When she ate

Szechuan chicken, we did, too; when we had hiccups, she felt every tremor. Out of the womb, we technically had a separate existence from our mothers. But of course the infant is no less dependent than it was before being born; in some respects, it's even *more* dependent. The comfort and sustenance that came effortlessly while floating in the womb now require a little individual effort: a suckle, a thumb in the mouth, an earsplitting, colicky cry.

Through these tiny efforts, the child begins to distinguish itself as a separate entity in the world. Months pass. The independence grows. The child finds the lesson of peekaboo a source of endless fascination: A person can disappear and reappear! How cool is that? Soon the child makes the intellectual leap: *Whoa,* people don't disappear—they just go out of sight. Mom is gone now, but she'll be right back—mom, who used to be "me."

The child holds on to furniture and cruises around the great forest of the living room. He or she lets go and actually takes a solo walk. Babbling turns into syllables that are actually understood by the adults in the room. At around fifteen to eighteen months, the child recognizes itself in mirrors or photos. By two, the child learns that he or she *is* in fact a he or she. And it is at this moment that the child, after months and months of saying nothing but yes—yes to the breast, yes to a spoonful of Beech-Nut apricots, yes to mom and mobility and speech—learns to say no.

No is a word that comes with tremendous power. Any parent who has ever experienced a child going through the "terrible twos" will know just how intoxicating that power can be, for in one transformative moment, children begin to understand that they can have some control over the outside world.

And that's how the child now learns to view the world: inside, outside. A distinction is emerging in the child's understanding of his or her relationship with the immediate surroundings—an inner-world/outer-world divide that some psychologists call the body boundary. On one side is the child's own body and all its working parts. On the other side is everything else in the world that is *not* attached to the body. The significance of this recognition of physical separateness can't be overstated.

Still, it's only the first step. The next one is trickier. It can be a little more difficult to pinpoint exactly *when* it takes place for each individual child, but it's even more difficult to say exactly *what* takes place. This new transformation is psychological, and always profound.

It's the birth of the secret self.

THE SECRET LIFE OF THE CHILD

For more than a century, students of human behavior have observed that children generally learn the concept of secrecy around the age of four. Until this stage, children believe (without realizing it) that their parents know everything about them—and they're right: Their parents pretty much *do*. Even when children learn to say no, they still have no reason to think their parents don't have the same thoughts and dreams that they do—the same inner life. But as children learn to exert greater control over the outside world ("No! No! No!"), they begin to realize that they know some things about themselves that their parents don't. And in the broadest sense, a piece of knowledge that someone has that nobody *else* has is, by definition, a secret.

This is the beginning of the self boundary—a recognition of not just a physical individuality but a personal identity. From a psychoanalyst's point of view, the simultaneous understanding of secrecy and the first stirrings of curiosity about sexuality is no coincidence. By now the child has not only discovered his penis or her vagina—those built-in toys that are as entertaining as anything made by Playskool—but has also figured out which parent has what. Yet if all the child did was make that physical distinction, then the discovery of her or his own sexuality would just be an extension of the body-boundary concept. The child, however, also *thinks* about the difference.

What each child thinks is unique, but the overall logical process at this stage of development is not. It goes like this:

If the child has an identity separate from his or her parents, then the parents must have an identity separate from the child. (Peekaboo!) And if having a separate identity is equivalent to having secrets, then the parents must have secrets, too. And if one of the defining components of a child's secret life is his or her private parts, then the parents' secret life must include those private parts, too.

The child doesn't have to throw open the bedroom door and

catch mommy and daddy "in the act." Of course, sometimes children do stumble upon what Freud famously called the primal scene. But even when they don't, they have every reason to suspect that something is going on between mommy and daddy, and it doesn't even have to be overtly sexual. The parents clearly have a bond that doesn't include the child—or, perhaps more to the point, that *excludes* the child. "It's a grown-up thing," goes the patent adult nonanswer to the child's curiosity about certain matters. "You wouldn't understand."

But one day you will. This is the promise contained within these responses. *One day you will find out what the world is like.*

And so the child sets off to conquer the world. As children begin to separate from their parents, they develop relationships on the playground and in school. Secrets are not the only means by which the child navigates these new landscapes, but this age is nonetheless the time when the child discovers that with the manipulation of information comes power. One way to manage information to one's own advantage is to lie, and by the age of five most children have become adept at this. But lies carry a cost, and lead to hurt feelings and punishment and guilt. Far less burdensome is to withhold and trade information as if it were a pack of Pokémon cards—to traffic in secrets.

Secrets are not the same as fantasies. At this age, children spend a good deal of their waking time living in a fantasy world. They play dress-up, and doctor, and ninja. Their stuffed animals go on elaborate adventures. Their imaginary friends come for a visit. But fantasies are parallel worlds, not secret lives. Ask a child how Binny, the invisible friend from far away, is doing these days, and she'll tell you. But she won't tell you what she tells Binny during those visits—and *that* is the nature of secrecy.

At first the secrets that children keep from friends are benign, even "pleasant and positive," as the authors of one study of secrecy in children found. Perhaps not surprisingly, given that young children have only recently recognized the body boundary—learning that "what's mine is mine"—the content of the earliest secrets tends to concern possessions. Sometimes what the child secretly possesses is a physical object: a new puppy, a candy bar, a tree house. Sometimes it's information. Does the child want a best friend's birthday present to be a surprise? Have the child's parents given instructions not to let anyone know yet that mommy is going to have a baby?

As the child gets older, however, the reasons for secrecy, and therefore the contents of the secrets, go through changes that reflect emotional growth. One study found that a group of third and fifth graders were more likely than seventh graders to have secrets about possessions by a ratio of 7 to 1. For the seventh graders, though, one of the main motives for keeping or sharing secrets was a sense of shame—a category that included a friendship with or yearning for a member of the opposite sex. The authors of the study summarized the difference between the two age groups as a shift from being concerned about the ownership of things to being concerned about relating to other people and paying attention to social demands.

We might say that the child is growing up. Through the manipulation of secrets, the child has begun both to realize an identity separate from his or her parents' and to negotiate an identity within society. The next question for the child can only be: How far can I go?

THE SECRET LIFE OF THE ADOLESCENT

Adolescence, every parent of a teenager will wearily tell you, is a time of testing boundaries. That idea assumes a new meaning if the boundaries being tested are the ones that have been discussed in the previous pages: the body boundary and the self boundary.

The body boundary is certainly a big deal for adolescents. For a decade or so, the now-teenage body has been separate from the rest of the world. But suddenly the body has started sending a seemingly opposite message, one with an overriding hormonal urgency: Find a fellow body.

As is often the case, what's happening outside, physically, is an indication of what's happening inside, psychologically. At this point adolescents are straining to establish an identity that will separate them from their parents once and for all. If they could, they would hang a DO NOT DISTURB sign on their self boundary just like they do on their bedroom door.

From the point of view of parents, a child's final drive for independence can be terrifying, even if they manage to keep in mind that it's not only normal but necessary. And it is. It's healthy for a child to establish a separate identity, to make the final break, once and for all.

In some ways, this step is the whole point of parenthood: to create an independent person. Ideally, it would be a result that's as rewarding as it is inevitable. Still, for most parents it can feel almost like the loss of a limb, because, on a psychological level, that's what it is. A part of themselves is taking on a life of its own.

By now this process has been going on for a long time. Yet even as the child has used secrets to fill out the details of his or her own inner life, the parents have been able to take comfort in the fact that they know, if not everything about the child, at least a lot, and certainly what's best for the child. In adolescence, though, the message that children have for their parents is exactly the opposite: *You don't know me at all.*

And it's true—not entirely, but true enough, especially as rebellion accelerates. Adolescents have sex; alter their states of mind, chemically or otherwise; pick a different religion from their parents; adopt a radically different approach to living daily life; dress in ways their parents never would. They fall in love with someone who replaces the parents—someone to whom they now confide their secrets.

With rebellion comes risk, a factor that teenagers are not always equipped to recognize. They actually *lack* the physiological equipment necessary to make sound judgments. The particular part of the brain that controls reason, the frontal lobe, is still developing throughout the teen years. That's why teenagers tend to want what they want now, without considering the consequences for tomorrow.

I know something about this, not only from my practice as a psychoanalyst, but also from my own adolescence. During the CB craze of the 1970s, I was a young teenager. Citizen-band radios were sort of like the 1970s version of Instant Messaging. You could adopt a handle—a fake name—and surf the radio frequencies until you found another human voice. My father had set up a CB radio in the garage, and I used to sit out there in the evening and do exactly what my parents had told me never to do for as long as I could remember: talk to strangers.

To those strangers I was "Sweet Talker." Amid the oil stains and gasoline fumes in my parents' garage, behind a door I always made sure to lock, I could transform from the adolescent I was into a sophisticated grown woman. I could do my best impression of what I imagined it was like to be a member of the adult world out there. "Worldly," in fact, is exactly what I thought I was during my anonymous chats with strangers, as though I were sitting in a smoky bar with a cocktail in front of me, laughing and talking easily to men.

The entire experience was titillating and thrilling. Or at least it was until the evening that a trucker began pressing me on where I lived. I told him what big city I was near, and he pressed a little harder, so I told him the name of my suburb, and he pressed a little harder still, because, hey, what do you know, he was in the neighborhood. Why didn't he drop by?

I sat there at the CB console, staring at the microphone and the wire that served as the umbilical cord to my secret identity. I had come so far—not just in this conversation, and not just in my role as

Sweet Talker, but in my new life. Creating this secret version of myself had been important to me; it had seemed urgent, necessary. I wasn't my parents' little girl anymore. And while I wasn't really a grown-up yet, I was well on my way. Having come this far, how could I turn back now?

THE SECRET LIFE OF THE ADULT

Once the adolescent graduates from testing the adult waters—whether dangerously or not—to actually entering adulthood itself, secrets continue to exert a vital social influence. Concealing private information remains an important way to maintain separateness; revealing private information remains an important way to create intimacy. The difference in adulthood, however, is what is or is not being revealed: the identity that the adult has spent a lifetime creating.

Part of what can make the decision to conceal or reveal so important is the information itself. The greater the secret, the greater the conflict: the greater the desire to give it away *and* the greater the fear of its exposure. What happens when you instruct yourself to keep a thought secret is similar to what would happen if someone instructed you to not think about white elephants: You'd think about white elephants. And the harder you'd try to not think about white elephants, the more you'd think about white elephants. Which would make you try harder not to think about white elephants, which would make you think more about white elephants, which would make you try harder, which would make you think more, and on and on. For the secret-bearer, the conflict between concealing and revealing can provide a psychological tension and urgency and stimulation not so different from the physical need to urinate, defecate, or reach orgasm.

"Confession is good for the soul," goes the old adage, for this very reason. The catharsis of revealing a secret can alleviate a great deal of stress and even relieve physical symptoms such as headaches, backaches, and so on. It can also provide a fresh perspective, letting the secret-sharer see that the secret can have different meanings for different people.

But it's not just the meaning—the content, the information itself—that invests a secret with its importance to both secret-giver and secret-receiver. It's the very fact of it. Even seemingly idle gossip carries a message: Out of all the people in the world with whom I could share this information, I choose *you*.

Sometimes the emphasis in this message is on the exclusive nature of the secret. Just as with keeping a secret to oneself, so sharing the same piece of information with a group can be a way of maintaining separateness. Membership in a secret society like Skull and Bones, or in a tony country club, is alluring precisely because it's exclusive. Passwords, handshakes, rings, and winks: These are ways for each member to say: "I choose you, and you, and you—and together we are one great big *not-them*."

But sometimes the emphasis is on the *inclusive* nature of the secret. By extending one person's inner self outward to someone else, a secret represents an offer to jointly create a new "self." It's an invitation to intimacy.

As with all invitations, it can be rebuffed. Going on national television and admitting a homosexual crush on a friend, as a guest on the old *Jenny Jones Show* did, probably wouldn't have been a good idea anyway, but the guest's literally fatal mistake was choosing a "friend" who would do what he later actually did: kill the lovelorn confessor. That's an extreme case, but life is full of potentially traumatic examples. A daughter's revelation to her mother that she'd been sexually molested by her father can produce sympathy for the daughter and rage at the father, or vice versa, depending on the mother and what she's willing to hear. Telling a new lover about having once been raped as a teenager can lead to comfort and understanding, or else rejection. Disclosing a medical condition such as cancer on a job application can result (however illegally) in not being hired, while an admission of being HIV-positive can lead to social ostracism. The mother trying to articulate to a member of the clergy the depth of her grief over the death of a child isn't helped by hearing, "God has His reasons." All of these negative responses speak more to the discomfort or prejudices of the person on whom the secret is being bestowed than to the comfort of the secret-revealer. These rejections pervert the situation by helping the *confidant* feel better, rather than the confessor. Worse, they can also reinforce a traumatized person's already low sense of self-worth.

Trusting in a different confidant, however, might have led to a different outcome, perhaps even a life-transforming one. Under different circumstances, these confessions might have been variously met with sympathy, acceptance, forgiveness, understanding. They might have led to the creation of a new, larger, united self, one that would have been stronger than the secret-giver's own individual identity.

A new self is in fact the foundation of any friendship. It arises out of the mutual disclosure of secrets, and it creates a landscape where those individual pieces can remain intact, free of criticism or resentment. When that pact falters, the friendship dissolves. But when that pact doesn't falter, the friendship flourishes.

And when you find someone in whom you can confide *all* your secrets, and who in turn can confide *all* his or her secrets in you, then for the first time since infancy you will have found a person who seemingly knows *everything* about you, and that is what we might call love.

THE SECRET LIFE OF THE MIND

So far, only one type of secret has been under discussion: the garden-variety, information-that-I-have-that-you-lack type. This is the conscious secret, the one that we knowingly decide whether or not to keep under our own hat. But there's another kind that figures largely in everyone's lives: the secret we unknowingly keep from ourselves.

To distinguish the thoughts we unknowingly hide from ourselves from the thoughts we knowingly hide from others, Freud adopted the term *unconscious*. Just like conscious secrets, unconscious secrets can be absent yet active. They, too, "want" out. And they get out, somewhat. They give themselves away through slips of the tongue, dreams, so-called innocent jokes. But they can also take more troubling forms: fantasies that seem contrary to our character, behavior that seems bizarre and otherwise inexplicable.

Fantasies in and of themselves are neither good nor bad. They don't make the person who has them good or bad, either. They just make that person human, because fantasies arise out of secrets, and to have secrets is to be human. Adult fantasies are simply variations on those of a child playing with stuffed animals or inviting Binny the invisible friend over for a picnic. While adult fantasies might differ from childhood ones in terms of appearance, their underlying content is similar, because the underlying secrets are the same. Anyone who's seen a child play with a stuffed animal, tossing it across the room, say, rolling around on the rug with it, or dropping it from the "cliff" of a table ledge, has witnessed acts of aggression and sexual sublimation. It's not the fact that fantasies exist that matters; it's what we do with them.

Consider me as a teenager, calling myself Sweet Talker and sitting in front of that CB radio in the garage. Now consider Adrian, the outcast who became a constant IMer. When my situation got too intense, I left the CB radio and went straight to my parents. Adrian, however, went to a parking lot in the rain to meet a man named chai83, who did indeed have black hair and blue eyes, but looked a lot older than he said he was. He was a stranger; he could have been anyone. She was, by all accounts, a girl who came from a loving home, raised by parents who had taught her right from wrong and instilled in her the importance of common sense. She must have known that traveling to a distant location to meet a man she'd encountered online, all the while having told no one where she was going—not her mother, who was clueless, or her father, who was well-meaning but unavailable, or her one or two friends, who had no experience in this kind of matter and wouldn't understand—was a dangerous thing to do. There was no way she could have overlooked the risks, and yet she went anyway, as if hypnotized.

Why did I know enough to back off when my adventure in anonymity got too intense, while Adrian didn't? What were the differences between us that sent us off on such different paths at the moment that a secret life reached a critical juncture? Both of us certainly had a conflict between our drive to *do* something and the inhibitions that told us not to do it. But desperation helped propel Adrian to take such a wild risk, and all sense of self-protection was immediately buried beneath it.

In her own life, she felt she was nothing, worthless, a loser. Her self-esteem barely registered, and she was convinced that she would never fit in, and that no one would ever love her. As she had written plaintively in the diary her parents discovered after her murder, she felt certain that no one even *liked* her. She did have a few friends, but something awful and embarrassing had happened at school that year, and she hadn't gotten over it.

Adrian had arrived at her locker after math class one morning in February to find a folded piece of loose-leaf paper wedged inside. It was a heartfelt note written by a good-looking but quiet boy who sat across from her in social studies. He wanted to know if she would meet him at the ice-skating rink on Friday night at eight; he was too shy to ask her out in person, he said. She didn't need to say yes or no, he instructed; all she had to do was show up.

Adrian was startled by the note, but she was also thrilled, and after dinner on Friday she grabbed the ice skates and pink skating skirt she never used, and headed for the town rink. The place was packed with teenagers gliding across the ice in clusters, and the music churned. Adrian stood by the entrance to the rink in her skirt and skates, looking for the boy, but he wasn't there. She waited awhile, and still he didn't come.

At first, she couldn't understand what had happened. And then, after a moment, she knew. Over in a corner, carefully watching her and poking one another and laughing at the high hilarity of it all, were the three meanest girls in the grade. With a sickening feeling, she suddenly realized that they had forged the note. They had set her up, and now they were reaping the rewards of their nasty joke.

It was a few days after that humiliating night that Adrian first began to talk to strangers on IM. The way to get the cool girls to stop being so mean to her and start paying attention in a good way, she wrote in her diary, was to show them that she was somebody. To demonstrate that a grown man, an actor with black hair and beautiful blue eyes, actually liked her. Her IM relationship with chai83 seemed as though it might accomplish this feat. It gave her a sensation of being appreciated, even loved. She'd been lonely far too long; her life was all about being excluded, and maybe now all of that would change. In addition to the devastation of being left out, Adrian likely found that the fantasy of being with an older boy, someone who even qualified as a "man," also satisfied a deep and essential need that had been there as long as she had been the yearning daughter of a handsome and distracted father. If Adrian had talked to a friend about her feelings of exclusion and hurt, and her desire to be part of the social world at school, she might never have needed to channel her feelings into an unhealthy and dangerous outlet, and perhaps would have declined chai83's invitation to meet in person.

Adrian and my teenage self were guided by different forces, and while I was able to let go of my secret life before it took over, she was not. At some pivotal point, her secret life became her real life, and then, finally, her real life was abruptly ended.

The reasons that anyone's secret life takes over differ from person to person, from secret life to secret life, from unconscious secret to unconscious secret. In every case, the answer lies in the conflict between the need to conceal and the need to reveal that unconscious secret. Actually, to be more precise, the answer lies in the lack of resolution of that conflict. Just as a conscious secret can generate great anxiety in the secret-keeper—and it probably did for Adrian, who was excited by her secret relationship but also perhaps uneasy—so can the unconscious secret, which in Adrian's case, was: *I am worthless, and I need a man to give me value*. If the anxiety doesn't find a healthy outlet, it will find an unhealthy outlet. But it *will* find an outlet, somewhere or other, and in the case of the thought that's secret even from the self, the outlet will be the creation of a secret life. In the end, the white elephant will not be denied.

[3 • THE SECRET LIFE OF EVERYONE]

A mirror that lies
A mirror that lies
That couldn't be me in the gorilla disguise.

—Steve Goodman, "This Hotel Room" (alternate lyrics; 1975)

Scott, a patient of mine, was a software "evangelist" whose work sent him out on the road a lot. He didn't mind, really, though his wife, Lisa, was less than thrilled at how often he was away. Their sons were young, and when Scott was gone from home the onus fell on Lisa to take care of everything. By telephone she would tell Scott what he'd missed that day, and he would murmur his involvement and concern. But really, he felt distant in more ways than one. The sealed window of whatever Four Seasons or Hilton he was staying in overlooked the lights of some city that wasn't his own. At night, all the lights looked the same. His wife's voice was tiny in his ear, and the words she spoke seemed somehow generic. He heard "kids," and "science project," and "car pool," and he went on automatic pilot, stretching out on the king-size hotel bed and closing his eyes, half listening to what she said, his thoughts curling out like tendrils that crept away from her and their sons and home and everything familiar. But his free-form thoughts didn't really have anywhere to go. He wasn't a particularly imaginative or visual man, and he found himself met with a kind of pastel blankness and dullness, not unlike the framed seascape on the wall above his bed.

One night, around 10 P.M., he realized he wasn't at all sleepy. Room-service dinner had been the highlight of the evening, but that was hours ago, and now the table had been wheeled out of his room, taking with it the momentary pleasures of the expense-account prime rib and stuffed potato. The scotch he'd poured from the minibar had left him with only the vaguest buzz. There was nothing to do now, and he didn't like that.

Scott flipped around the channels on the TV and briefly considered, then rejected, paying for Nintendo. If his kids saw him with a joystick in his hands, they would call him a hypocrite, because he was always telling them to shut off their video games and read a book. They were almost never in the mood to read. He wasn't either, at least not right now. He let CNN drone on for a while—something about a drought in the Southwest—and then he watched ESPN, which featured the highlights of a college basketball game he had no interest in, and finally he turned to the menu of pay-per-view movies.

"Adult titles," read one of the choices. He'd seen it before, in hotel room after hotel room, but on this occasion it caught his eye in a new way. "Why not?" he thought. "What's the harm?" So there he was, within thirty seconds, watching a movie that featured two big, blond, farm-girl-type women having sex in a hayloft. Their moans were extravagant and fake, but it didn't matter; he was hooked. He was a guy, and he reminded himself that guys liked this kind of thing, and so he gave in to the moment, with all its hammy theatrics and false lesbianism on display for a bored forty-year-old husband and father in a hotel room.

Suddenly Scott was no longer bored. The remote control fell from his hand onto the bed. His mouth opened slightly like that of a fish trying to breathe out of water, and he worked open the belt that Lisa had bought him for his birthday and found himself completely absorbed by the pornography that was scrolling in front of him on a TV screen in Portland, Oregon, three thousand miles from home. He had seen plenty of porn in his time, but for some reason he hadn't felt this excited since he was an adolescent and got a look at Susan Cahill's naked breasts in the rec room of her suburban house.

When the movie was done, and his orgasm had been achieved with great swiftness and a quiet yelp of pleasure, in near synchrony with the manufactured orgasms of the on-screen farm girls, Scott fell right asleep. He woke up in the morning feeling rested and oddly happy. It was as though something unusual had happened to him on this business trip, but he knew he couldn't tell his wife about it. What was he supposed to say: "Hey, Lisa, guess what, I got off on soft-core porn last night, and now I know how to amuse myself when I'm on the road"?

No, he wouldn't tell her; not that she'd really mind, anyway. Most women accepted the fact that men's brains were different, that they responded primarily to visual stimuli. He'd read that in a magazine recently. And he reminded himself of that convenient fact the next time he found himself spending a night in a hotel room. Fairly soon, watching soft-core porn became a habit Scott indulged whenever he traveled. More than a habit, actually. During the day, discussing software, delivering PowerPoint presentations in conference rooms, he would find himself looking forward to his evenings alone—those evenings that until recently had felt so lonely. Even when he was back at home, playing with the kids or helping Lisa make supper, he would find himself thinking about the next road trip and his new ritual. As soon as he walked into a hotel room now, he would check out the movie offerings and plan his evening accordingly. He'd eat dinner, get himself a drink from the minibar, put himself into a state of relaxation, then watch *Hot Girls of Rio* or *Nights in Wet Satin,* or whatever was there for the taking.

You pad the expense account. You bad-mouth a coworker. You resent your mother. You just happen to pack the hotel towel. You feign interest in your best friend's child's kindergarten play. You declare a tax deduction that might be legit . . . or might not. You covet a dress, scheme to be prom queen, take steroids while training for the Olympics. You turn on the porn channel, and then you turn it on again.

The point is, *you* do these things. *We* do these things. *Everybody* does these things.

Not *all* these things, of course; it would be difficult to imagine that every one of you reading this book is a cheating Olympian who covets your neighbor's dress while lying to a kindergartner. But the fact is, every one of us does keep secrets, and each of us does so on a daily basis.

Keeping secrets, of course, can be healthy. Keeping some secrets can be essential. By keeping secrets, we create our inner selves—the identities we develop in early childhood and carry inside us throughout our lives. Eventually the secrets we keep also serve as the core of the shared self—the adult identities we hope to create with a partner. Throughout our lives secrets provide a foundation for friendships and business partnerships and social alliances.

Even when keeping a secret isn't life-altering, however, it can still serve a useful purpose. The friend's child who has the lead in the kindergarten production of "Cinderella" wants praise, not the naked honesty of an opening-night critic. The wife of an executive who finds his new secretary "hot" probably doesn't need to hear that today the next Jessica Simpson walked into his office. If Scott's encounter with the porno channel had been nothing more than a "one-night stand," he very well might have seen no reason to confess his "infidelity," and his wife, Lisa, very well might have agreed.

Such secrets are *benign*. They don't hurt anyone, and in fact they might spare someone else's feelings or help secret-keepers feel better about themselves. They might serve perfectly sound purposes.

Shades of gray, however, can quickly crowd the canvas. The executive who finds his new secretary hot might find his mind wandering toward her even while he's having sex with his wife. From a psychological standpoint, such thoughts are neither moral nor immoral; they're merely understandable. Fantasies are not behaviors and are not harmful. They're benign. And if the secret-keeper acknowledges the existence of the secret, rather than denies it, the secret will tend to stay benign. The same is true if the secret-keeper doesn't think the secret is actually solving a problem—marital dissatisfaction, a midlife crisis.

But what if the executive asks the secretary out for coffee? What if he doesn't happen to tell his wife about this tête-à-tête? What if he confides in his secretary some intimacies that he hasn't shared with his wife? Now the secrets have begun to take on a more sinister cast. If the secret isn't understood as a fantasy that need not be acted upon, isn't being acknowledged by the secret-keeper for what it is, and is solving a problem or conflict that exists in the secret-keeper's mind, then it might spread. Such a secret we can call *malignant*.

Where do malignant secrets come from? The seven deadly sins

are a good place to start: vanity, envy, anger, greed, sloth, gluttony, and lust. They were designated as potentially "deadly" to the eternal soul by the sixth-century pope Gregory the Great. Apart from their religious significance, these seven categories have endured for a millennium and a half in Western culture because they represent what are probably the most common and most resonant temptations of the heart. It is important to point out here that every human being does and will think about and feel every one of these urges. (And anyone who believes he or she doesn't think about or feel these urges is likely repressed in the extreme and probably consumed with guilt.) In that sense, there's nothing "sinful" about any of these thoughts and feelings. By knowing that you think and feel them, and by struggling internally with these thoughts and feelings, you can prevent yourself from doing something that could be wrong for you or someone else.

Even so, malignant secrets carry only the *potential* to spread. They don't *have to* metastasize. There's a world of difference between the Starbucks barista who dips her hand into the venti-size tips box once and her store manager, who regularly makes 5 percent of the week's profits melt away like so much cappuccino foam. Likewise, tourists who have taken towels from hotels are legion. But they can't hold a scented candle to the chronic continent hopper whose powder room is stocked with the spoils of world conquest: towels, to be sure, but slippers, too, and toenail clippers, and test-tube-size samples of shampoo, and mood CDs, and a white-noise clock, and a four-cup coffeemaker, and a closetful of hangers (wooden!).

The difference between secrets and secret lives is one of degree. This difference might not be strictly quantifiable. How many nights did Scott have to charge pornography to his private credit card in order to be officially leading a secret life? You can't simply assign a number to it. Yet like the classic Supreme Court definition of pornography, you might know it when you see it—which was one reason Scott made sure nobody did see it, including himself. Like most people, Scott tended to see himself in a flattering light, and he preferred that the world perceive him in an equally favorable fashion.

In psychological terms, this somewhat idealized version that a person carries around inside himself or herself is called the ego. Scott wanted his family and friends to regard him as a moral, stable, fun, faithful, and sexually well-adjusted guy. He didn't want them to glimpse the weary husband and father lying on a bed on the eighth floor of a hotel in downtown Minneapolis, getting off on watching pseudo lesbians wrestle in a hayloft. He didn't even want strangers to see him that way. Whenever he checked out of a hotel and a clerk presented him with the printout of the bill, Scott would feel a flush of embarrassment working its way upward from his semistarched collar. The titles of the movies never appeared on such bills, of course; instead, the charge would be listed as something like "In-Room Movie." Yet as far as Scott was concerned, his bill might as well have read

"Pornography for Middle-Aged Businessman to Masturbate To." On the whole, Scott preferred the convenience of express checkout.

Besides, that *wasn't* him. That couldn't be him, this image that family and friends and associates and strangers would conjure up if only they knew the truth about Scott. What's more, it wasn't even really accurate, he told himself. Like most keepers of malignant secrets, Scott preferred not to admit that the vision of him lying fevered on the bed or feeling furtive in the lobby was who he really was. He had his reasons: He was bored; spending night after night in generic hotel after generic hotel would drive anyone to distraction; men's brains simply work this way, only he was late to discover this scientific fact for himself; and anyway, who wouldn't need to unwind after a stressful day trying to convince a roomful of middle-management types that the latest software tweak could make a significant difference in their company's bottom line?

But then, secret-keepers always have their reasons—their rationalizations. The office worker helping herself to a pair of scissors or the pharmacy customer who decides not to tell the cashier that he's handed back a ten-dollar bill instead of a single can tell themselves that their little pilferings don't matter. After all, the multinational conglomerate where they work or the national drugstore chain where they shop can easily absorb such a minuscule loss. They somehow "forget" that the companies are owned by human beings, and that those human beings will either personally absorb the loss or pass it along down the line to other human beings who will personally absorb the loss. And by forgetting, these petty thieves depersonalize their dishonesty and maintain their favorable self-image.

But what they are *are* petty thieves. Their "take" might be minuscule, yes. But moral? Someone who wouldn't dream of shoplifting a printer cartridge or pocketing a penny accidentally left behind at the drugstore counter by the previous customer, might act on an impulse that's going to cost somebody somewhere some money. But these petty thieves take what they take because they can—because nobody else is in the supply closet at the moment, or because the cashier doesn't realize his mistake. Nobody is watching them, except themselves. They take it because it's there for the taking. They're getting away with something. That feeling gratifies them because it satisfies a primitive urge. Life's unfair, but this time the unfairness works out in their favor. In that moment of crossing the line, petty thieves—malicious gossips, tax cheats, drunk drivers—are not *only* moral, upstanding, honest citizens. They might like to think of themselves as being moral, upstanding, honest, and they might be right. That impression of themselves might be entirely accurate—or almost entirely, anyway. Because at some level, inside each of us, we're also aggressive, amoral little beasts.

In psychological terms, the part of a personality that wants what it wants, wants it now, and doesn't concern itself with consequences is called the id. It's the impulsive, selfish, survivalist side of human nature. It is the version of our inner selves that becomes visible when the flattering light of the ego goes dark.

Freud used to write about the id as if it were an actual physical part of the mind. Today we use the word to express a concept about the way the mind works. But if you want to imagine what the id might look like, just think of the Internet. You want something when you want it? Google it. You want to be completely anonymous, or adopt another identity altogether? Go to a chat room. You want to rant? Blog. Some of the secrets that the Internet makes universally accessible are benign—the pseudonym you use for your e-mail address, or the identity you adopt in a chat room. But some lend themselves to malignancy—to hate speech and predation. Incognito, the id can run wild and free.

The battle between the ego and the id—between the image of ourselves that we want to present to the world and the more sinister image we try to harbor out of sight—lies at the heart of the malignant secret. We want to be the person we most want to be, but we want what we want, too. Often, the ego wins this battle. You leave the cartridge in the supply cabinet at work; you return the ten-dollar bill to the cashier who meant to give you a single. At other times it's the id that wins—and sometimes, the id *should* win. It's emotionally healthy for the id to get some satisfaction. If you harbor lustful thoughts and if thinking them provides some release, then in that particular section of your life the id will have found not only an outlet but a *necessary* outlet. Keeping the id fully buttoned down can create a repressed, resentful, inhibited, rigid person who has no fun and is no fun.

But while *wanting* to grab the cartridge from the supply closet or leave the pharmacy with the ten-dollar bill can be healthy, actually doing so is not. If the battle between id and ego is not fought consciously and thoughtfully, then you might behave in ways that are harmful to yourself or others. Wanting to get rid of your boss can be healthy. Recognizing that you want to get rid of your boss can be healthy. But *not* recognizing that you want to get rid of your boss and then spilling coffee on his desk is not healthy. If an impulse that you feel strongly enough to act on is kept unconscious and left unexamined, then the id might not only win but keep on winning.

When that happens, the malignant secret has begun to spread. The towel packing becomes a routine part of travel. The cartridge stealing leads to scissors, tape dispensers, reams of paper, boxes of pens and pencils, and whatever else the kids at home need for their school supplies. The in-room porno movie becomes a nightly affair. And when *that* happens, the rationalizations have done their job. They've allowed the secrets to take on a life of their own.

Because she had always been "bad at math," it was easy for Sarah to remain ignorant about taxes. Jason dealt with them, not her. She did meals, kids' orthodontia appointments, and homework help, and he did taxes, garbage, and car. Not very enlightened, but there it was, and it worked for them. Every year, a couple of weeks before April 15, Jason, an executive at a major investment company, took all their earnings information into the den, closed the door, and didn't appear for many hours, at which point he looked utterly wiped out. Because he had a background in finance, he told Sarah they didn't need to pay an accountant to do what he could do for free. He prided himself on his expertise; he'd come from a working-class background and had been the first person in his family to graduate from an Ivy League university, and he was still proud of how far he'd come and how much he knew about the world. She never questioned his judgment, but just let him take care of things, which he seemed to do so well. Jason would hand her all the IRS forms to sign, and she would sign them.

Once, though, her eye happened to fall upon the list of itemized deductions, and she saw that he had included their recent trip to Turks and Caicos, calling it a "research" trip for a project she was working on. She couldn't imagine what he'd meant by that, but he waved off her concerns, saying that everyone took those kinds of deductions, and the IRS knew it. Also, she couldn't find any mention of a part-time freelance designing job she'd done in the summer, but when she brought this up, he dismissed those concerns, too, saying the income was "in there somewhere," and that she just didn't know how to read tax documents.

Which she didn't, to Jason's relief. Over the years, he read up on how to bend the truth on his income-tax statements, and by the time he was thirty, it was nearly a science. No one needed to know what he did with those numbers; no one needed to know the way he made them dance to his advantage, not even his wife, Sarah—though he had a feeling she knew a lot more than she was letting on.

As a family, they had everything they wanted: the BMW, the country home, the obscenely large plasma TV. Sarah loved their life, and would never want to change it. She easily recalled the old days, back when she and Jason had nothing. He was fresh out of Penn, spending his days going to job interviews and trying to impress the heads of personnel with his combination of working-class street smarts and Ivy League polish. They ate cheap, greasy Chinese takeout then, and lived in a small apartment. They were optimistic that they would soon be able to change their lifestyle, and sure enough, they were. Jason proved to be a valuable employee who knocked himself out and rose rapidly, becoming a senior vice president at his company. Everything was perfect—at least until the day the envelope from the Internal Revenue Service arrived in the mail, informing them that they had been selected for an audit.

The secret life that Jason and Sarah shared was one that they had chiseled together out of two separate secrets. For Jason, the secret had begun with some simple stretching of the truth—a questionable deduction here, an implausible omission there. He could rationalize every entry he made on every line of every tax form. Cloistered in the den, his fingers flying over a calculator keypad, he would amuse himself by anticipating the questions of an imaginary auditor, and he always had a good answer. He wasn't a tax cheat. He was a guy who happened to understand finances in a way that few people could fathom. He had a perfect right to locate and exploit every last loophole, and if his expertise should happen to fail him on occasion and he wound up making a mistake here or there, who could blame him?

Jason's secret in turn came to envelop Sarah. When she first glimpsed the possibility that her husband was cheating on their taxes, she told herself that it couldn't be true. But then the more she thought about this idea, the more difficult it was to dismiss. So she didn't think about it. If Jason told her that everything added up, then everything added up. Sarah cloaked herself with what politicians call plausible deniability: She couldn't be held responsible for something she didn't technically know for sure . . . right?

Her secret in turn came to reinforce Jason's secret. When Sarah signaled that she not only had some awareness of what he was doing but was also willing to look the other way, Jason interpreted her response as an acceptance of sorts, a suggestion of "How bad can it be?" Not bad at all. The system was working. Everyone was happy. Through their collusion, one man's secret was elevated into a family's secret life.

This is the way family secrets often work. One person's secret life spreads outward, seeking reinforcement, demanding collusion. And if the potential rewards of the secret seem to match the unconscious desires of the other family members, the secret will flourish. It will become part of the household. It will be *normalized*. Even a secret life as extreme as Tony Soprano's is normalized through the collusion of the other members of his household, who all depend on his being a mobster to satisfy their id-driven desires for money and status.

But what if an everyday secret can't be normalized? It might be difficult to imagine a secret life more resistant to normalization than Tony Soprano's. But what decides whether the person with the secret needs the collusion of his family isn't the secret itself. It's the secret-keeper's own feelings about the secret.

People keep malignant secrets for basically two reasons. One is the guilt, which is the feeling (valid or not) that you have done something wrong. The other is shame, the feeling (valid or not) that someone else might think badly of you. So if you're wondering whether a particular secret of yours can be normalized, then the questions you can ask yourself would deal with these two issues. Does this secret make me feel guilty, ashamed, humiliated? Would another person who knew my secret judge me as bad, corrupt, disgusting, weird, amoral? If you answer yes to either or both of these questions, you'll probably feel the need to keep the secret to yourself, regardless of what the secret is. For you, such a secret is one that might never be normalized.

Being skinny as a reed was something Shelly had always taken for granted. Her body was long and slender, and throughout her childhood and adolescence she never put on any extra weight, no matter what she ate. Then, to her astonishment, her skinny-reed days ended. She was twenty-seven at the time, and her clothes began to feel snug. Shelly vowed that if she still wanted to look attractive, she would have to watch what she ate. But it was hard to diet after a lifetime of never having to do so. She would be fairly strict with herself, then eat a forbidden doughnut, telling herself it really didn't "count," because she'd eaten only salad the day before.

Then Shelly started hoarding food from the fridge, taking it into her room when no one was around. She began a drastic pattern of bingeing and purging, convincing herself that such extreme measures were temporary. She also changed her style of dress from clingy and trendy to loose-fitting and conservative, covering up her expanding body. Shelly told none of her friends or family about her weight gain, or about her tactics for dealing with it, but fervently hoped that somehow, none of them would notice.

Of course, they did notice. Which turned out to be a good thing—and perhaps a lifesaving thing. Her friends urged her to get help, and after entering therapy with me, Shelly began to confront her weight problems directly. She came to see that the more she tried to repress disturbing thoughts about herself and her body image ("I look disgusting," or "No man will want to sleep with me if I'm overweight"), the more likely she was to act them out in subtle or not so subtle ways. She came to understand that she had been using food as a means of comfort, one that replaced real human, sensual contact. Without knowing it, she had been eating so much because she was actually *scared* of sexual attention and physical intimacy. Her fears had depressed her, which made her more likely to overeat, which made her feel more depressed, which made her more likely to overeat, which allowed her to avoid the threat that sex presented. Shelly had achieved exactly the opposite of what she'd set out to accomplish.

The same was true of Jason and Sarah. Jason's creative accounting would sometimes rise to the surface of his consciousness for what it was. And Sarah would sometimes glimpse her husband's dishonesty and recognize her own willful ignorance. And sometimes each of them would see the possible ramifications of what was happening; they would realize that they were jeopardizing their family and their future. So horrific was this scenario, however, that like innocent bystanders in a movie who have just witnessed a mobster commit a murder, Jason and Sarah would tacitly agree that they'd seen nothing out of the ordinary.

Only they *had* seen it, at least fleetingly. But they could afford to "forget" it as long as they believed that doing so was in their best interests. In Shelly's case, she couldn't help but see her own secret every time she looked in a mirror or walked past a shop window. She even went so far as to recognize her need to disguise it. But she still managed to pretend to herself that she *didn't* see it, and that therefore nobody else would see it either. Shelly used a kind of childlike "magical thinking" to keep this logic alive.

In the end, Jason and Sarah saw their secret life for what it was only because they were *made* to see it. When the IRS came knocking on their McMansion door, they had no choice but to recognize that something had gone spectacularly wrong in their lives. They wound up owing the government tens of thousands of dollars, and they had to sell the very possessions that had sustained their illusion of prosperity. Each blamed the other, as is often the case when couples have colluded on a secret life that comes to light. But then came the day that Sarah said, "We need help." Jason immediately snapped back, "Yeah, a good lawyer," but she told him that what she had in mind was a therapist. Even then Jason resisted, protesting that the problem wasn't in their heads but in their bank account. Eventually, however, the clear and present threat of divorce—of losing his wife and family—got through to him in a way that the distant possibility of prison or the actual loss of property had not.

When I asked Jason why he cheated on his taxes, he said he was just trying to "stick it to" the government. But further discussion led to a deeper understanding of his defiance. When Jason was a teenager, he'd had a summer job on the loading docks of Brooklyn, and on payday he would come home with cash folded in his jeans pocket. He distinctly remembered the sensation that those pieces of paper engendered, rustling near silently against the denim. He felt tough, he recalled; he was invulnerable. But then not long after he came into the house, his father would always corner him and demand the cash, saying that he would put it into the bank for Jason, where it belonged. "I'm just trying to be prudent," his father always explained. "And teach you the value of money." Jason had learned the value of money, all right; after a while he always made sure to hide some of his earnings from his father, stuffing it in a sock in the drawer. It wasn't the government he wanted to "stick it to" as much as it was his father or any figure of authority.

When it was Sarah's turn to explain why she had been willing to overlook her husband's lawlessness, she shrugged and said she wanted "a good life" for herself and her family, like the one she'd had as a child, growing up in an upper-middle-class suburb of Philadelphia. Only after much further discussion did she realize that "a good life" was also what her parents feared a Brooklyn dockworker would never be able to provide for their daughter. Not that her parents had actually voiced their reservations. But she could hear their heavy sighs over the phone whenever she spoke of Jason, and she could see their forced smiles when she and Jason spent the holidays at her parents' home. *I'll show them* became Sarah's own unspoken vow. Every extravagance she added to her household, every luxurious vacation she planned for her family, was a way of proving her parents wrong.

We might be tempted to say that, unlike Jason and Sarah, some people cheat on their taxes because they feel they have no choice. April 15 nears and they discover that the fifteen-thousand-dollar windfall that looked like a blessing in the winter now looms like a curse. Wouldn't a little cheating have nothing to do with the unconscious?

No. Each person responds to each situation in an individual way. Not everyone who comes up short on April 15 would cheat on their taxes, no matter what. And those who do, do so for an unconscious reason.

We also might be tempted to say that Jason had an abusive father, Sarah had judgmental parents, so *of course* they turned out this way. Shouldn't that reassure those of us who didn't have abusive fathers or judgmental parents?

No. We all have malignant secrets, but malignant secrets wind up metasticizing only because we keep secrets from ourselves. Together Jason and Sarah kept a secret from the outside world, and individually they kept secrets from each other—creative bookkeeping on his part, pretending not to notice on hers. And their complicity had worked, for a while. They had created the life they wanted. But because they also kept secrets from themselves—because they had never acknowledged their deeper secrets—they engaged in the very behavior that destroyed the life they wanted. Like Shelly fearing that she would become unattractive and then indeed making herself unattractive, Jason and Sarah feared that they wouldn't be prosperous—and in the end, they weren't. The unconscious, unaddressed secret can easily become a self-fulfilling prophecy.

And what about Scott? He, too, wound up defeating himself. He had begun watching pornography on the road out of loneliness, a sense of isolation, and soon he was lonely and isolated at home, too. The effort of keeping his habit a secret made him irritable, even unreasonable. He would find himself comparing Lisa, the living, flawed woman in his bed, with the big-breasted, perfectly tanned twenty-year-olds on a TV screen in Kansas City, and there was no competition. The secret he was keeping from Lisa was sending him further and further away from real closeness with his wife. He felt *false* now. When he was home between business trips, sitting at breakfast with his wife and kids, or lying in bed beside Lisa at night, he was aware of a strange sensation of detachment—not only from his family, but also from himself. He was reminded of a scene in *Annie Hall* in which Diane Keaton's character makes love with the Woody Allen character, and in the middle of the act she appears to get up from the bed and walk around the room while another version of herself stays in the bed and continues making love. The only time that Scott didn't feel as though he were observing himself from a distance was when he was on his own, watching porno in an anonymous hotel room. The secret he was keeping from Lisa was starting to dismantle his marriage. And because Scott had never acknowledged the underlying reasons for his behavior—the unconscious secret he kept from himself—he arrived at a "solution" that only made matters worse.

What that solution was, and how his story eventually resolved itself, will have to wait until the final chapter of this book. Until then, here's a cliché, but it's an apt cliché, because it's one that always applies to a secret life as long as the unconscious secret at its core remains unexamined: *to be continued.*

[4 • THE SECRET LIFE OF THE LOVER]

Get the butter.

—Marlon Brando in *Last Tango in Paris* (1972)

His visits were infrequent, brief, and memorable. Up to three times a year, the tall, handsome, English-speaking man would materialize in the Munich home of the three Hesshaimer children. He called himself Careu Kent, and judging from the sheaf of papers he often carried, the children assumed him to be a famous writer. They knew he was a world traveler, anyway; they would overhear him talking to their mother about the famous people he knew, such as Richard Nixon. Then, in 1973, his visits stopped. Another eight or nine years would pass before Astrid, the middle child and by now twenty-one, discovered a box of 112 love letters to her mother, all signed, not surprisingly, *C.*

What *was* surprising was the subject of a magazine article that her mother had carefully stored in the same box: Charles Lindbergh.

Astrid confronted her mother. Brigitte Hesshaimer, by then in her midfifties, confirmed nothing and denied nothing. Instead, she broke down crying. Then she elicited from her daughter a promise not to say anything about the letters publicly until after her own death, as well as the death of Charles Lindbergh's legitimate widow, Anne Morrow Lindbergh.

Both women died in 2001. In the summer of 2003, the three Hesshaimer children—Dyrk, forty-five; Astrid, forty-three; and David, thirty-six—went public with the letters. They provided photographs of the aviator with the family. They also supplied details of their domestic life.

He amused them by wiggling his ears. He displayed a tolerance for waking up in the morning and finding puppets stuffed in his oversize shoes. He spoke no German, but through pantomime he could thrill them with stories of the animals he'd seen in Africa. During his visits, which routinely lasted five days to two weeks, he would often take the three children and their mother on excursions to the countryside. He had bought their mother a house, and he had provided trust funds for the three children.

The conclusion, they said, was inescapable: The line on their birth certificates that read "Father unknown" could now be completed with the name of one of the most famous figures of the twentieth century.

The conclusion seemed inescapable to *them*, anyway. To the rest of the world, this private image of Charles Lindbergh was virtually irreconcilable with the public image: disciplined, strict, moral, a devoted father and a loving husband. Even the foremost Lindbergh experts said the claims of the three Hesshaimer siblings couldn't be true. Biographer A. Scott Berg took one look at the letters and agreed that the handwriting was Lindbergh's. But did the references to "our children" in the letters necessarily mean that Lindbergh was the father? Berg had gotten to know Lindbergh's character as well as anyone, and he said that in all his research he had detected "not an inkling" of such a possibility. "Is it chronologically and geographically possible? Yes," Berg said in an interview. "Does it sound true to his character? No."

Lindbergh's public persona included the status of hero, the first person to fly solo across the Atlantic Ocean, a feat that, in 1927, at age twenty-five, elevated him to the highest echelon of international celebrity, where he remained until his death forty-seven years later. His public identity also included the status of tragic hero, following the kidnapping and murder of his three-year-old son, Charles Jr., in 1932—a case that captured as much attention as had the solo flight.

And then there was his private character—those traits and details known mostly to a person's partner, but also, somewhat, to a small circle of family, friends, and, in Lindbergh's case, a biographer. By all accounts, Lindbergh's private side suggested a core of iron—stern, unemotional, and uncompromisingly moral.

Yet however seemingly untrue to Lindbergh's character, a depiction of him as a polygamist was nonetheless factual—to a 99.9 percent degree of accuracy, according to a DNA analysis conducted in the fall of 2003. And the story doesn't end there. Soon after Lindbergh's three children by Brigitte Hesshaimer made their claim public, a German magazine revealed that Lindbergh had fathered two other children—with Brigitte Hesshaimer's sister, Marietta. A short while later, another publication uncovered yet another secret family of Lindbergh's, this time one he started with his German secretary, Valeska. This secret life, too, included two children.

When Dyrk, Astrid, and David Hesshaimer published a book about their father two years after they first went public with their story, they called it *The Double Life of Charles Lindbergh*. By that point, however, a more accurate title might have been *The Quadruple Life of Charles Lindbergh . . . and Counting*.

If Charles Lindbergh had settled in Munich with Brigitte Hesshaimer and raised three children, and *only* settled in Munich with Brigitte Hesshaimer and raised three children, nobody would have thought his private life unusual. The difference between the secret life of the lover and the open life of the lover, however, is that the *secret* life of the lover involves another person—"another" as in "an other," a new other with whom to establish a new identity.

It might begin with a throaty laugh, or an accidental brush of the back of a hand across a wrist, or just the fact that the other person is good-looking. Maybe it's a well-told joke, or a keen insight, or a compatible political opinion. Whatever the particular trigger might be, the secret life begins right there.

It might well end right there, too. It often does. The thought flickers to life, encounters an inner resistance—perhaps a loyalty to the primary partner—and dies.

But sometimes it doesn't. An exchange of pleasantries might follow. A flirtation, too, perhaps. At this point, both parties might be proceeding under the assumption that while some manner of a mutual attraction exists, the relationship isn't "going anywhere"—that it's not leading to a romance. And as was the case with the initial trigger, maybe it won't in fact go any further. A friendly if secretly meaningful flirtation might be as far as this new relationship gets.

Then again, it might not. These flirtations might be just what the soon-to-be secret lover has been looking for, a reprieve or a release or even a way to escape an existing relationship. Or maybe the appearance of a possible new "other" comes as a complete surprise, calling into conscious existence an unasked, perhaps previously unthinkable, question: *What if?*

Consider even the best-case scenario, in terms of emotional fulfillment. A couple connects through the sharing of secrets, each of their inner selves revealing itself more and more until eventually the two separate selves merge into one shared self. Each inner self gives and gives and gives, and gets and gets and gets, the two of them spilling their guts and opening their hearts until there's nothing left to spill or open. Then what?

For some people, that's enough. But for others, who, knowingly or not, want more, what follows can be a bit of a letdown. After the first headlong rush toward mutual fulfillment, stagnation inevitably sets in. Sometimes this is accompanied by a diminishment in sexual activity. This period doesn't have to coincide with a so-called midlife crisis, the kind that comes complete with growing children, pressure-cooker careers, parents in need of care, receding hairlines and advancing cellulite, or any other reminders of lost youth or impending mortality. It can happen at any point in life, and it can be subtle enough to escape notice. But it can create a vague and undefined suspicion: Something is missing.

What in particular might be missing is beyond the scope of this book. The fact is, something is always missing. Not to put too fine a point on it: That's life. We all know all too well our own individual inadequacies and frustrations and anxieties and fears. To feel incomplete is part of the human condition. Once, though, it wasn't. In infancy, we ideally experienced a oneness with a parent or parents. Now, by establishing a oneness with someone else, we hope to reclaim some semblance of that blissful state of completion.

So far these descriptions of a developing relationship could apply equally to an open love life and a secret love life. First comes an implicit recognition of attraction, then an explicit recognition through flirtation, then an accelerating exchange of emotional intimacies, and finally, the distinct possibility of sex. The possibility of sex, however, raises two further possibilities: the physical affair and the emotional affair.

In the 1972 film *Last Tango in Paris,* the characters played by Marlon Brando and Maria Schneider repeatedly meet for sex in a vacant apartment. The only ground rule is that the sex must be anonymous; the two characters must reveal nothing about their personal lives, not even their names. In effect, by removing secrets from the equation, they hope to erase their humanity, at least within the four walls of this one room.

Even so, can such a scenario really remove human intimacy? After all, an individual declaration of a preference for one type of sexual act over another reveals something intimate to the partner. From a psychoanalytic perspective, it also reveals something key. The message that such a preference sends is: "Something is missing, and this is what I think can replace it—or at least, for the moment, satisfy me in its absence." In the case of Brando's character, we learn that what's missing on a literal level is his wife, who has just committed suicide. But in a pivotal scene, he stands over his wife's coffin and berates her in language so vulgar and with a rage so naked that it's clear his anger goes much deeper than his feelings toward this one dead woman. He's a fictional character, of course; it's always dicey to try to reach too far into a nonexistent psyche. But if he were real, we might wonder if his inner conflict involved his relationship with women in general—a "missing" piece of him that dates back, as troubles with women often do, to his mother. In terms of the psychological reality of the film, it's not surprising that shortly after this scene, Brando's character reveals his name to Schneider's character—a revelation that signals the end of their affair.

Which is not to say that anonymous sex can't exist or doesn't exist. (Though even the desire for anonymity—the pursuit of sex without revealing secrets—can be telling.) But in relationships where both parties seek any degree of emotional intimacy, sexual acts convey a powerful amount of information. Sex involves parts of the body that we're not supposed to show anyone, a form of pleasure that we don't tell anyone else about, fantasies that speak to our deepest longings. For these reasons, it serves within our society as the final frontier in intimacy, the one irreversible course of action. It's as if the integration of two self boundaries isn't symbolically complete until there's been an integration of the body boundaries, an exchange of secretions validating an exchange of secrets.

But what about the inverse of sex without intimacy: intimacy without sex? Not only does it exist, but it happens all the time, and probably more frequently than ever now that changes in the workplace and the rise of the Internet have made casual meetings (virtual or otherwise) between the sexes more prevalent. But can an emotional relationship that doesn't involve sex actually qualify as an affair?

Yes. What defines an affair isn't necessarily sex but secrecy. A deep exchange of secrets serves as the foundation for intimacy, and such intimacy *can* lead to sex. But it can also lead to a nonsexual but equally compelling and consuming relationship: an emotional affair.

Julia met Stephen during a smoking break outside the office building where they worked for competing advertising agencies. It was a cold day, and they made the usual small talk about how crazy they were to be standing outside without coats on, and then they tamped out their cigarettes and went back inside. To Julia, it didn't seem that Stephen had been flirting with her, the way men often did. She always made sure to mention that she lived with "a great guy." But this time it was Stephen who had gone out of his way to mention his wife, as if to reassure Julia that he considered this casual meeting simply a pleasant way to pass five minutes in the cold. But the next day Julia and Stephen happened to meet again during a smoking break, and then they arranged to meet the next day at ten-thirty and three-thirty. "If we're both going to be cold and miserable . . ." Stephen said, his voice trailing off.

"Misery loves company," Julia agreed.

But Julia didn't feel miserable at all. In fact, she felt invigorated, a feeling that had nothing to do with the cold. She honestly enjoyed talking to Stephen, and it turned out they had a lot to talk about—the kinds of advertising clients they really liked or really hated, deadline pressures leading up to major presentations, frustrations about the prospects for professional advancement within their respective agencies. Julia even found herself confessing her innermost professional ambition—to be head of her own boutique agency one day. She'd never told anyone that secret, not even Bob, her longtime lover. "R U miserable?" soon became Julia and Stephen's secret e-mail code to meet downstairs whenever either of them needed a smoke—or wanted to see the other.

Before long Julia had agreed to meet Stephen for an after-work drink, and then another the following week, on a Wednesday. By now the subject of an affair was unavoidable, and they both declared they weren't interested in having one. They loved their partners. Just because they happened to be members of the opposite sex who enjoyed each other's company, they agreed, didn't mean anything had to "happen." Why can't two people like themselves just be friends? After all, if they were two men or two women, there might be no question of their intentions.

Yet something didn't feel right. No, something felt *too* right. Julia felt an ease with Stephen that she didn't experience even with her closest friends—a sense of comfort she hadn't felt since she'd fallen in love with Bob four years earlier. Sitting in a banquette at a quiet midtown bar, ordering another drink, asking to see a menu, Julia felt comfortable, understood, *appreciated*. Which, she told herself, wasn't necessarily a bad thing; now she didn't need to demand or expect from Bob the kind of support their busy lives and, frankly, their longtime familiarity no longer allowed. But Julia also had to wonder: If her friendship with Stephen wasn't in fact such a bad thing, then why wasn't she telling Bob about the specifics of her Wednesday evenings? Saying she was "just stopping off for a drink with this friend from work" was true, but it wasn't the whole truth, and somewhere in the landscape between the truth and the whole truth lay an increasingly guilt-ridden minefield.

Julia was beginning to realize on her own that a nonsexual emotional affair could be just as potent, just as consuming, as a sexual affair. In general, if someone can answer yes to at least two of the following questions, then he or she is probably having an emotional affair:

1. Do you keep most meetings and conversations with this person secret from your partner?
2. Do you tell this person more about your day, or even about your marital dissatisfaction, than you do your partner?
3. Do you ready your appearance before seeing this person?
4. Is there a sexual attraction (spoken or unspoken) between the two of you?
5. Would you feel guilty if your partner saw the two of you together?

On her fifth Wednesday evening out with Stephen, Julia said that this had to stop, whatever "this" was. The term *emotional affair* wasn't yet in her vocabulary, but she now had firsthand experience with what being involved in an emotional affair feels like, what threat it poses, and what its repercussions are. In Julia's case, what lingered afterward was an unshakable sense of guilt, one that grew so strong she eventually sought the help of a therapist. Only then could she begin to accept that for a brief but intense period, she had been living the secret life of a lover.

Even while poised on the brink of an affair, potential adulterers can still step back. They can still try to determine whether whatever it is that feels "missing" is absent from the relationship or from themselves, and they can also try to figure out how to find it without jeopardizing their primary relationship. They can still go home and try to figure out what, if anything, is wrong.

Sometimes something within the relationship *is* wrong, undeniably and irreversibly so. Certainly many relationships have run their course by the time a third party enters the equation. And certainly some relationships *should* end, for the sake of sanity or even safety. For someone who either has previously recognized or has only now come to understand the need to get out of the primary relationship as soon as possible, the arrival of an "other" can indeed be a blessing and a solution.

But in many cases the secret life of the lover is born of the belief that *any* relationship might be able to fulfill a longing for completion.

And how acutely a person experiences this longing will affect how likely he or she is to adopt the secret life of the lover. To paraphrase Freud: What do women and men want?

Generalizations about gender can be hazardous, unless they're of the "men have penises and women have vaginas" variety (and even then there are exceptions). Still, experienced psychoanalysts and psychotherapists can identify broad distinctions between where women and men hope to find that sense of completion.

Women in general tend to hope it will come from the "other." They'll think, "He wants to be with me. He loves me, he desires me, and therefore I am lovable and desirable." Women tend to see a relationship in terms that are more emotional than physical. The sex with the secret lover might be fine, but it's the attention and appreciation that carry a more important message: *This man makes me feel desirable, funny, smart*—unlike the way the man at home makes her feel. This particular observation of hers might not be objectively true. She might in fact have a lover at home who's deeply appreciative of her but for whatever reason doesn't show it anymore. Nonetheless, a sense of fulfillment is what she feels is "missing" at home—and it's what she hopes she can get from another lover.

For men, the search for the sense of completion tends to lead them right back to themselves. They'll think, "I want to be with her. I want her, and I want to want her—I like what wanting a woman and getting a woman say about me." Men tend to see a relationship in terms that are more physical then emotional. The emotional component of the relationship might be fine, but it's the sex that carries a more important message: *This woman makes me feel like I've still got it*—which just might be what the woman back home makes him feel, too. But it can't hurt to hear it again, right here, right now. What a rush—to feel adventurous, vital, virile.

Consider Lindbergh. We can only speculate as to what his unconscious motives were—what the actual reasons for his behavior were. But his example can serve to illuminate larger truths. In his case, potency certainly seems to have played an important role. By 1957, the year he began his affair with Brigitte Hesshaimer, he was fifty-five and his wife was fifty-one. Together they'd had six children (five surviving), the youngest of whom was then twelve. What's more, they'd lived through the death of a child, in the 1932 kidnapping. Perhaps Lindbergh had a psychological need to reassure himself.

But he didn't just reassure himself. He reasserted himself. Since he had at least seven children out of wedlock, we can safely conclude that he didn't exactly discourage the conception or birth of these living, breathing testaments to his virility. In fact, if what he wrote to Brigitte is to be believed, he welcomed her letter (received, anonymously, at a post office box in Connecticut) informing him of the imminent arrival of their firstborn. "The news you send is wonderful, and I am tremendously happy about it," he wrote to her (sent, anonymously, in an envelope without a return address). "I just wish I could be there with you now, instead of writing this letter."

So where did his sense of incompleteness, his unconscious desire to replace something that was "missing," originate? A good place to start thinking about it is his upbringing. Lindbergh's father was himself the offspring of an extramarital affair between a Swedish farmer and a mistress thirty years his junior. By having his own affairs and fathering his own illegitimate children, perhaps Lindbergh was unconsciously trying to hang on to his father by, in effect, replicating him. We also know that Lindbergh was raised by a mother with a strict sense of right and wrong, and that she carried herself with a formality that extended even to bedtime, when she would shake her son's hand good night. No doubt such rigorous childhood discipline at least to some extent helped him endure thirty-three straight hours alone in the cockpit of a plane crossing the Atlantic, keeping himself awake by dipping the plane just low enough to touch the whitecaps and spray ocean water in his face. And that discipline also eventually allowed him to compartmentalize his life to such an extent that he could have at least four distinct families.

Not surprisingly, this rigidity—moral, physical, psychological—also extended to his emotional life. According to his wife, he never once shed a tear in her presence; even after the death of their son, he forbade her from shedding a tear in *his* presence. The message he learned from his mother must have remained with him for the rest of his life: *I mustn't share my emotions with anybody, and they mustn't share their emotions with me.* What was "missing" from Lindbergh's inner life, we can safely say, was true intimacy.

Just as it requires a conscious effort to keep an affair secret from the rest of the world, so it requires an *unconscious* effort to keep this kind of secret from *oneself*. Secrets—conscious or unconscious—want out. And they get out, one way or another. It is not only the outer, conscious desire that determines whether an affair happens. It is this inner, unconscious conflict that also drives a lover into the arms of another.

And another, and another, in the case of Lindbergh. The secret he kept from himself was the need for intimacy, and so he felt compelled to embark on a series of affairs to fill that void. But all someone so emotionally distant is capable of initiating are pseudo intimacies.

True intimacy comes about when two identities merge. Each identity is the inner self that emerged in early childhood, as the individual person began to distinguish himself or herself from his or her parents. Now, as an adult, that individual inner self seeks to return to that merged state, though not with his or her parent. Now the inner self seeks another inner self with which to make one shared self. In order to reach that stage—in order for the two identities to achieve true intimacy—each inner self must be willing to surrender unconditionally to the other.

The unconditional surrender that leads to true intimacy as an adult, however, is not an option for someone who didn't experience the unconditional surrender of true intimacy as a child. But that doesn't stop such a person from searching—from trying to find that certain "missing" something.

In the case of Lindbergh, he never experienced true intimacy with his mother. So, as an adult, he sought that certain missing something first with one lover, but he didn't find it there, so he sought it with a second lover, but he didn't find it there, and then with a third lover, but he didn't find it there, either. He was never going to find it. But such was the nature of his demons that he was doomed to try and fail, to try and fail, to spend the rest of his life going through all the traditional motions of falling in love without once understanding what it was he really wanted and how to get it. The last decades of his life must have felt, emotionally speaking, like one long solo flight.

It says something about how desperate to fill a void secret lovers must be if they are willing to risk so much. They are willing to jeopardize their relationships with wives or husbands, with their children, with other family members, and sometimes, if the social transgression is extreme enough, even with friends and coworkers. The affair doesn't even have to be exposed to have its pernicious effect. Lindbergh, for instance, never formally abandoned his American family, but he certainly left his wife and children behind. Although he maintained his primary residency in Connecticut for the final fifteen years of his life, he was constantly traveling, constantly absent, to such an extent that Anne Morrow Lindbergh complained in her diary that she already knew what it felt like to be a widow.

For Lindbergh, the close relationships he was jeopardizing extended to an adoring public. The same year he began his affair with Brigitte Hesshaimer, the movie version of his autobiography was released. The Charles Lindbergh of *The Spirit of St. Louis* was even more heroic—more steadfast, moral, disciplined—than the Charles Lindbergh the public already knew. In public, he found himself growing from a hero to a myth, an icon, a god. In private, he was willing to take the risk of becoming a pariah, a hypocrite, a fake. Then again, who can say how much of a risk he was taking? Maybe by this point in his life he would have (on some unconscious level) welcomed exposure. It might have been a relief, the righting of a wrong that would have appealed to the moralistic side of himself.

For reasons secret lovers don't understand, they can find themselves behaving in ways they don't countenance. Lindbergh prided himself on knowing right from wrong, yet he serially committed an act that not only violated prevailing mores but was surely one he once would have considered immoral (and maybe still did). Not only would the public not have recognized this Charles Lindbergh, but Charles Lindbergh wouldn't have recognized this Charles Lindbergh.

Or should we say Careu Kent? Certainly a figure as famous as Lindbergh needed an alias if he was going to keep an overseas affair secret, especially one that resulted in children and required regular visits. But the name he adopted is itself possibly revealing of his inner conflict. In the German countryside, he could fancy himself to be mild-mannered C. Kent, yet as that name suggests, he remained at heart a "Superman" who could leap, if not tall buildings in a single bound, then at least wide oceans in a nonstop flight. He was someone who could swoop down occasionally and bestow his presence on his lovers and their children, and then fly off again. It would have been a pattern of behavior that suited his superhero version of himself while also allowing him to believe he was approximating real intimacy. He could be physically present from time to time, and financially responsible, but he was also a specter as emotionally present, or absent, as his mother had been. If that assessment seems harsh, just remember: He put on wild-animal pantomimes for the children he fathered with Brigitte Hesshaimer, but he needed to do so because *he never bothered to learn German*.

Who would put up with this kind of behavior? Part of feeling compatible with a partner is finding someone who complements one's peculiarities, and in Lindbergh's case, he needed to find women who would acquiesce to their lover's lengthy absences from their own lives as well as those of their children. And the kind of woman who would do that is almost by definition one who would accept him unquestioningly, who would place few if any demands on him emotionally, who would idolize him: *Look! Up in the sky!*

Once the truth about Lindbergh's double life became irrefutable, his biographer Scott Berg noted that only now could "those holes in the story" be filled. The holes in Lindbergh's chronology were there all along, puzzling to a biographer but not overly worrisome. Without the knowledge of the letters and the parallel lives, even his biographer could continue to make sense of the life of Charles Lindbergh. In the same way, the holes in Lindbergh's inner life were there all along.

They, too, must have been puzzling to Lindbergh: temptations and needs and impulses that contradicted not only who the public thought he was, and not only who his wife and children and friends and even his biographer could believe him to be, but what he consciously knew of himself. In the end, Charles Lindbergh couldn't make sense of his life, and, as is the case in the secret lives of many lovers, that inability—that duplicity—was as "true to his character" as he could possibly be.

[5 • THE SECRET LIFE OF THE HOMOSEXUAL]

Daphne: "You don't understand, Osgood. (He removes his wig.) I'm a *man*."

Osgood: "Well . . . nobody's perfect."

—Jack Lemmon and Joe E. Brown in *Some Like It Hot* (1959)

Jim had wanted to be a Marine for as long as he could remember. From an early age he also knew he was gay, and instinctively he understood that the two parts of his life would be in conflict. When he went off to join the Marines, he told no one that the person waiting for him back in Duluth was a man named Michael. All during his tour of duty in Vietnam, Jim sent love letters to Michael in care of Michael's sister, Susan. In fact, everyone in his unit thought Susan was his girlfriend, and this deception made life much easier.

After Vietnam, Jim remained a career Marine, and he rose through the ranks until eventually he occupied a position of some prominence. He regularly attended diplomatic dinners in Washington, where politicians and other VIPs were always happy to see him. They would grasp his hand firmly and clap him on the back, as if meeting an equal. He knew he was admired, and he liked being admired, and he especially liked being admired for performing a service for his country. So he would mingle with other guests, listen to the toasts with them, talk about the Redskins with them. And then, later in the evening, after he'd left the dinner and stopped by his apartment for a change of clothes, he would drive over to a bar called the Grotto.

Jim always insisted that he'd made his peace with his double life. He acknowledged that it could be wearying to have to guard himself at all times. But he was a Marine; he was good at discipline. Besides, he knew about living with risk on a daily basis. He'd been in battle.

One day, Jim came into my office visibly shaken. He told me that a good friend of his had been outed by another Marine, just like that, and though Carl was only nine days shy of retiring, he was stripped of his pension. His life was ruined, and he was left with nothing. This sent a wave of fear through Jim and, he said, through the knot of other gay guys he knew in the Marines. If it had happened to Carl, it could happen to them, too. None of them were safe.

I reminded him that he'd always insisted he knew the risk he was taking by being gay in the military, just as he'd known the risk he was taking by being a soldier on a battlefield.

"I guess it's one thing to know you might die out there," he answered softly. "It's another to have a bullet graze your ear."

Dodging a bullet is an apt metaphor for the way many homosexuals have to live their lives. Those completely or only somewhat in the closet fear exposure. Even those completely "out" risk retribution. Gay men and lesbians might not be consciously aware of these concerns every waking moment. They might routinely make their way through society as if they were "equals," just as Jim felt when he mingled among the politicians, diplomats, and military brass at Washington dinners. But there remains in the life of some homosexuals a constant unspoken, unseen threat—a pressure from the outside. And it is this need for secrecy imposed from the outside that can make daily life for someone on the inside seem very much like a battlefield.

Even in the supposedly nonjudgmental arena of psychiatry, homosexuality was long treated as something to be "cured," and if a patient was "converted" to heterosexuality and got married, the treatment was considered to be a success. We know better now. Homosexuality isn't a choice, as we thought, and the medical professions don't view it in terms of morality, either. The thinking now is that, in at least the vast majority of cases, it is the result of some sort of biological predisposition. It's what one is born with. "So show me the gay gene," goes the counterargument. There is no one "gay gene." No one can yet say what particular genetic or neurological component determines sexuality, but clinicians throughout the mental-health professions now agree that people are "hardwired" sexually.

Not that sexual preference is simply a matter of an on/off, heterosexual/homosexual switch. We aren't either one or the other. We all fall somewhere along a continuum—many of us much further toward one end or the other. But none of us occupies one unambiguous, absolute extreme, because an attraction to the same sex is, to some degree, part of everyone's historic sexuality.

It may not be the *predominant* or *conscious* attraction. Still, at various points in childhood, a person will be attracted to his or her mother, then the father, or vice versa. Eventually one type of attraction will dominate and the other will become repressed and therefore unconscious. That's why some individuals maintain the capacity to be attracted to both sexes even as one predominates. For example, a heterosexual woman might see another woman walking down the street and think about how sexy that other woman's figure is. In part, this response might come from admiration or even competition. But she also might be feeling, if only she could admit it to herself, that she finds the other woman attractive, even really *hot*. This doesn't mean she wants to sleep with her, or with any other woman.

Sexual preference can also be determined in part by psychological factors. Someone who feels a deep conflict with or aversion to the opposite sex (because of being sexually abused as a child, for instance) might find members of the same sex "safe," no matter what his or her natural sexual orientation might be. Some people experiment sexually as a way of testing social boundaries, often in late adolescence or early adulthood. And then there are those who are predominantly attracted to members of the same sex but find those thoughts so horrifying that they suppress their natural tendencies, even to themselves, and even unto marriage. But people who are gay as adults overwhelmingly report that they had always been attracted to members of the same sex, that their fantasies always involved members of the same sex, even in grade school—that they always "knew."

"I Am What I Am" was a song from the early 1980s Broadway hit *La Cage aux Folles*, and it was also an anthem for the gay-rights movement of the time. But part of the poignancy of the song was that for many gay men and lesbians, the opposite of the title was true: "I Am *Not* What I Am." What you see—this straight "me" you think you know—is not the person I am inside. Of course, nobody is exactly the same on the inside as on the outside; the secrets we choose to keep are part of what give each of us an individual sense of self. But to someone partially or wholly in the closet, the secret being kept is not minor or peripheral in the least. It's not about one aspect of a life. It's central to that life. It is the essence of *anyone's* identity: the way we love.

When Jim the Marine eventually fell in love, his attitude toward the military and his own homosexuality shifted in a decisive way. For years his fellow Marines—or at least the straight ones—had always assumed he was just a very private person. They thought he was a "loner," a "confirmed bachelor," and he did nothing to disabuse them of this notion. But once he fell in love, he would leave a diplomatic dinner at, say, the French embassy, and head not to the Grotto but home, and instead of experiencing the high of thinking he'd outwitted all the dull and probably bigoted people he'd left behind, he felt sad. He and Craig would tell each other about their days, as couples do at the end of the day, but as Jim told Craig what he'd missed that evening, he experienced a growing indignation. Dodging a bullet was one thing; discrimination, he was beginning to feel, was another. Why shouldn't he be able to bring his lover to these dinners, the way other men brought their wives or even their girlfriends? Or, as he once asked me, "How does a mistress outrank my boyfriend?"

We live in a society where being homosexual is still, in many straight people's minds, a source of shame, and, in some gay people's minds, a reason for secrecy. As a result, the construction of the secret life of the homosexual is always at least partly a response to external pressures.

When Roy Scherer was offered a chance to be a Hollywood leading man in the 1950s, he probably didn't hesitate long before agreeing to studio demands that he hide his homosexuality and adopt the almost comically masculine pseudonym of Rock Hudson. In that era and in that industry, a public disavowal of homosexuality was routine. In this particular case, it included "dating" a succession of starlets. For Rock Hudson, his new identity became so much a part of who he was and how he wanted to be remembered that even as he lay dying of

AIDS in 1985, he reportedly admitted his homosexuality only with great reluctance.

By contrast, Rosie O'Donnell eventually came out as a lesbian, and then solidified that identity further by marrying her girlfriend in San Francisco when that municipality briefly legalized same-sex weddings. Before then, however, she had cultivated a wholesome, everywoman image among her talk show's predominantly female audience in part by proclaiming as frequently and as forcefully as possible how attractive she found Tom Cruise. And you know what? Tom Cruise *is* attractive. She probably *did* find him attractive. It's just that male handsomeness wasn't her predominant source of sexual interest. For her, as she later acknowledged, pretending that it was simply seemed professionally safer.

She was right, in a way. Consider the case of Ellen DeGeneres. Unlike Rosie O'Donnell, she had never publicly declared her sexuality one way or the other. Then, when rumors about her began to surface, in 1997, she took to the cover of *Time* magazine and famously declared, "Yep, I'm gay." At the same time, her sitcom character also came out. However beneficial her honesty might have been to her own psychological health, it didn't help her professionally. Her sitcom quickly disappeared, and so did her career. Not until the movie *Finding Nemo* opened in 2003 did her professional life begin to recover—perhaps in part because she was giving voice to an unassuming fish that, while a girl, seemed to be of no discernible gender and certainly conveyed no sexuality. And although she soon found significant success as a talk-show host, she did so while not making her lesbianism part of her public identity. The lesson of her experience was clear: It's still not professionally safe for a beloved public figure to admit being gay. (For a sex symbol, it's probably career suicide.)

There are further gradations of gay identity in show business. There was the "don't ask, don't tell" approach of Liberace, as flamboyant a showman as has ever graced a stage, yet somehow thoroughly nonthreatening to his core audience of elderly women. And there's the "no way, so it's okay" tradition of straight playing gay—or, in the classic 1959 comedy *Some Like It Hot,* straight playing straight playing gay. Technically, Tony Curtis and Jack Lemmon's characters are cross-dressing musicians on the run from the Mob, not gay men. But there is also, in the movie's final moments, the definite suggestion that one of them will be running off with a wealthy old playboy. For its day, that ending was subversive, but it was also acceptable because the audience knew that the actor playing the role, Jack Lemmon, wasn't "really" gay.

Examples from show business are useful for our purposes because they're visible and they're familiar. But homosexuality is probably more common in the arts than in many other walks of life. What's more, it's tolerated within the industry itself. For showbiz insiders, the news that Rock Hudson, Rosie O'Donnell, and Ellen DeGeneres were gay was not news at all.

In other fields, however, it's the industry itself that exerts varying degrees of pressure to keep homosexuality a secret. At one extreme is the intelligence community, which makes intolerance not only the norm but the official policy. The rationale is that homosexuality poses a security risk, because gay people with access to sensitive information are supposedly prone to blackmail. But as a 1990 paper in *American Psychologist* pointed out, homosexuals are prone to blackmail only because the culture of the intelligence community itself makes the revelation of their sexual preference compromising. If the intelligence community tolerated homosexuality, then the power of the threat of exposure through blackmail would disappear.

But even more to the point, the author of that same paper argued, being gay might actually make an applicant a better spy. Wouldn't closeted homosexuals be more adept at manipulating sensitive information? Lesbians and gay men learn to watch what they say and what they do. They learn to look out for social situations that might lead to being exposed or harassed. The paper's conclusion: "Experience with stigma may actually increase a gay applicant's ability to maintain secrecy." Perhaps it's no coincidence that when Valerie Plame's identity as a CIA operative was revealed, the word that the press frequently used, as though it were an official term, was *outed.*

The U.S. military is one place whose current attitudes toward gay men and lesbians reflect a kind of hybrid sentiment that exists in society at large. Though the armed forces continue a policy that forbids homosexuals in their ranks, since the early 1990s they have added on the muddled "don't ask, don't tell" mandate. What this seems to mean is that a gay person can be in the military as long as no one knows of his or her orientation. According to an extraordinarily thorough study in the year 2000 of 71,570 service members on thirty-eight military bases and eleven naval vessels, 80 percent reported having heard slurs against gays within the previous year, and 37 percent reported having seen or experienced harassment based on the perception (accurate or not) of homosexuality.

In other institutions, intolerance isn't the official policy, though it just as well might be. Gay men participating or officiating in major U.S. sports might not want to out themselves because of the risk of public ridicule—the same reason as their show-business counterparts in the movie industry. But in almost all cases they also know that they would suffer ostracism within the clubhouse or locker room.

At the community level, policies about homosexuality are usually arrived at haphazardly, in response to laws, local standards, and the beliefs or prejudices of the person heading the organization or department. Several studies have found that anywhere from a quarter to two-thirds of gay employees report workplace discrimination. Other studies have pointed out that these numbers, high as they are, actually might be misleading. They might not accurately reflect the *potential* for discrimination. Who knows what the level of prejudice or harassment would be if the closeted employees in the surveys were out at work?

Even in a relatively tolerant workplace, a gay employee might feel uncomfortable. What about the company's annual "family" picnic? How accepting is it, really? Would a gay employee feel comfortable bringing his or her partner? How would his or her supposedly open-minded coworkers respond? There can be a big difference between the abstract and the concrete—between knowing that the guy in the next cubicle has a male partner at home and actually seeing that partner at the picnic, hopping along in the three-legged potato-sack race.

For that matter, the family itself is an institution, and the levels of secrecy there can be just as labyrinthine as in any other institution—and often more so. There are families where only one parent knows, because the gay son or daughter believes that parent will be accepting and the other will not. The gay child and sympathetic parent wind up colluding, sharing the secret between themselves so as not to enrage the intolerant parent and risk splitting up the family. Sometimes both parents know and it's the siblings who are not told, and vice versa. And sometimes, of course, nobody is in on the secret, and the bachelor son (for instance) heads toward middle age fending off offers of blind dates from well-meaning aunts or overhearing the whispers of friends that "he just hasn't found the right girl yet."

And finally, it's possible to be out in one setting but not in another. A gay person can "pass" as straight in the workplace or at the family Thanksgiving dinner but have a same-sex live-in lover and a social circle in bars, restaurants, neighborhoods, and resorts where he or she can experience a sense of community otherwise lacking in life—or in the imitation of life, anyway.

"Always the bridesmaid, never the bride," Jill muttered as she got into her peach-colored gown on the morning of her sister's wedding. Jill's lover, Rachel, sat on the bed, watching her in the mirror. There was irony in Jill's remark; there often was, for Jill was considered a witty and funny person by all her friends. But there was melancholy there, too, and something in Jill's voice caught, and her eyes flooded.

Her moment of emotion wasn't about gay marriage per se. She didn't feel a burning need to get married. But the bridesmaid's dress just reminded her of all that had been denied her because she was a lesbian. Not only a wedding, but also the genial, easy approval of her large family—all the cousins and aunts who teased Jill's sister, Karen, about her handsome fiancé, and who loved to feel as though they, too, were a part of the relationship between the young couple.

For when you are in love, the world loves you back. You and your lover walk down the street arm in arm, and old ladies stop to smile, and construction workers whistle, and everyone applauds the openness and purity of what they know you have. Because they have had it, too, or at least they've wanted to have it. The world loves lovers, and this fact always enhances love itself. Especially in the beginning of a relationship, there are fields to lie in and kiss in, and bunches of flowers to carry home, and everyone around you knows the story, and applauds it.

For Jill, though, none of that applied. She was simply unable to tell her parents that she was a lesbian, though she'd known it since she was thirteen years old, when she fell in love with her best friend and dreamed about her every night. When, during sleepovers at her friend's house, the two girls had lain side by side in the twin cocoons of their sleeping bags and talked and talked, Jill had felt a kind of completeness that she later recognized as love. Such feelings would be repeated as she got older: She fell in love with a young woman in her art class at college, and a waitress at a sake bar, and then, finally, with the woman who lived down the hall from her in her new apartment building, who turned out to be Rachel.

But in each instance, Jill felt herself perpetually scoping out the situation, asking herself: "How real can I be in the world today?" If she and Rachel were in New York City for the day, she would allow herself to put an arm around Rachel. If she and Rachel were at one of Jill's family dinners, she would refer to Rachel as her "friend," and her mother would never have questioned that in a million years—though her brothers and sister knew. In fact, they thought it was funny, and smirked at her across the table, as though her life were a door-slamming farce in which some people knew, other people didn't, and everything had to be choreographed and navigated or it would all fall apart.

So that day, as she got into the bridesmaid dress, she realized she was dreading the wedding. Because here were all the different parts of her world—family, friends, neighbors, teachers, her minister—and while her natural desire was to show off her love in front of them—to shout it from the proverbial rooftops—instead she had to monitor herself. See who she was taking to, and who was around. "I'd like you to meet my friend Rachel," she would dutifully tell most of the people there. And some aunt would ask why such pretty young women weren't accompanied by dates.

Some of Jill's lesbian friends couldn't understand why she felt such pain at her inauthenticity. "Who cares if you can't tell your old aunt?" was their attitude. "You're in love, you're happy. What does it matter?"

But it did matter, because Jill came to feel that the inauthenticity tempered her love. She wanted a feeling of whooping freedom and expression, but so often found herself having to button it up. Her sister never had to do that. That day at the wedding, there would be all kinds of wink-wink toasts that alluded to the great passion between the bride and groom. Jill lay back on the bed, rumpling the dress, feeling a wave of envy.

"How real can I be today?" was a question that poisoned so many things in her life. She wondered, for a brief and sickening moment, if eventually it would even poison her love for Rachel.

How real can I be today? The question that haunted Jill is the one that every person living the secret life of the homosexual always has to ask. On any given day, there are as many answers to the question as there are people to answer it, for the pressure to keep one's homosexuality secret doesn't come only from the outside. It also comes from inside the individual.

Two homosexuals living in identical circumstances, responding to identical cultural and institutional pressures—two persons residing in the same community and even working in the very same workplace—can lead radically different lives. One might be out to everyone, at home as well as on the job, and the other might be closeted, even from an openly gay coworker. In psychiatric circles, we no longer try to "cure" a patient of homosexuality, but when treating a gay patient who is experiencing ambivalence about his or her sexuality, as was the case with Jill the bridesmaid or Jim the Marine, we try to address the internal conflicts—the pressures from *within*.

To be in the closet to everyone or totally out to everyone or some combination in between is ultimately a matter of individual circumstances and psychology. Some homosexuals are unconflicted about their sexuality. But far more report the need to maintain a delicate balance between ease in the world and authenticity. Not that the two are mutually exclusive. To be authentic—to be openly gay—can certainly make you feel more sure of yourself and therefore more capable of navigating daily life. But on other days and in different circumstances, it can also get you fired, divorced, ostracized, or killed. Answering the question of how real to be is often a matter of pride, shame, fear, guilt, and anger.

As with all secrets, this secret creates a desire to reveal and a need to conceal. The difference in the secret life of the homosexual, however, is that this cycle of revealing and concealing requires constant, conscious vigilance. Such self-monitoring is what determines how each individual answers the question "How real can I be today?" But it also, inevitably, takes an unconscious psychic toll.

Sometimes the internal response is to agree with the outside world's judgment: Yes, I should be ashamed, and I am ashamed. "I have decided to get married," the gay Russian composer Pyotr Ilyich Tchaikovsky wrote to his brother, Modeste, in 1876.

> It is unavoidable. I must do it, not just for myself but for you, Modeste, and all those I love. I think that for both of us our dispositions are the greatest and most insuperable obstacle to happiness, and we must fight our natures to the best of our ability. So far as I am concerned, I will do my utmost to get married this year, and if I lack the necessary courage, I will at any rate abandon my habits forever. Surely you realize how painful it is for me to know that people pity and forgive me when in truth I am not guilty of anything. How appalling to think that those who love me are sometimes ashamed of me. In short, I seek marriage or some sort of public involvement with a woman so as to shut the mouths of assorted contemptible creatures whose opinions mean nothing to me, but who are in a position to cause distress to those near to me.

Within a year, Tchaikovsky had indeed married. But because the strategy of "going straight" involves a denial of who a person is at a fundamental level, it is nearly always doomed, just as Tchaikovsky's was, though not to the same extreme. Within weeks of getting married, he attempted suicide, abandoned his bride, and fled the country.

Sometimes a gay person's response to the pressures of the outside world is to feel jealous, as Jill did. Or they might feel inspired to political action, as gay-rights activists have since the Stonewall riots in June 1969, when a group of gay men stood up to the police outside a Greenwich Village bar and sparked a social revolution. Both responses are variations on a more fundamental emotion: anger. After years of claiming he felt comfortable with his straight-by-day, gay-by-night existence, Jim the Marine fell in love and saw a close friend unceremoniously get kicked out of the armed forces. Only then did he tell me about a fantasy he'd been harboring all these years—that on the day of his honorable discharge, he would march up to his commanding officers and announce his homosexuality.

As he and I discussed this fantasy, Jim acknowledged that it contained a good deal of anger. Anger, he recognized, was in fact what he'd always felt. It surfaced in the way he sometimes confronted his superiors. Fortunately for him, his vocation accommodated hotheadedness. But Jim had been afraid to confess that anger at the military, even to himself, because he thought it would detract somehow from the pride he felt in serving his country. Only now that he'd addressed both his anger and his pride did he begin to see that they were separate issues. He could be angry *and* proud. Perhaps he couldn't be totally real on any given day, but by recognizing his anger, he could be more real than he had ever been.

For those like Jim who feel that a secret life is necessary yet impossible to acknowledge, a healthy outlet does exist—one that can encompass all their individual frustrations and longings, conscious and otherwise. Secrets emerge, only in disguised form.

This process is called sublimation. By taking a "bad" or socially unacceptable thought or feeling and turning it into something "good" or socially acceptable, the secret-keeper experiences relief—and perhaps, as in the case of Tchaikovsky's music, transcendence. It might seem paradoxical that his music could be so romantic, considering he was someone who didn't lead a particularly romantic life—unless you take into account the romantic longing that went into its creation. What is *The Nutcracker* ballet, if not a fantasy exploration of love? And *Swan Lake* tells of a young man who, under pressure from his mother to get married, falls in love with a beautiful woman trapped in the body of a swan because of a sorcerer's evil spell. While this story of thwarted love and transformation is in the tradition of many classic fairy tales, the subject appealed to Tchaikovsky because it addressed some of his deepest unrealized yearnings. Issues of love, identity, and disguise spoke to Tchaikovsky, as they often do to people who lead a secret existence. They resonated so deeply with him that he transformed them into music that resonates deeply with an audience.

Tchaikovsky understood that he was homosexual, despite his unfortunate attempt at a married life, and he understood that he needed to keep that fact secret. He understood that he felt pressures from society, and that he felt pressures from himself. But the combination of those pressures, from without and within, didn't defeat him when he sat down to compose.

Sometimes, however, the combination of pressures from society and pressures from within finds an unhealthy outlet. A gay man or lesbian might feel not just the kind of shame that drove Tchaikovsky to attempt marriage but an inward aggression that, at its most extreme, can take the form of self-loathing. Or a person sensing a homosexual longing can deny the existence of those feelings to such a degree that they manifest themselves instead as outward aggression, ranging from a habit of compulsively telling "gay jokes" to physical violence against homosexuals. And when the denial of homosexual thoughts and impulses is complete—when they have become impossible to acknowledge—then the secret life of a homosexual will be secret not just from others but from his or her own inner self.

Roy Cohn, the legendary power broker and influence peddler who operated at the highest levels of café society and government, apparently believed that regularly having sex with men didn't make him gay. But a secret interior life doesn't have to involve somebody actually having sex with another person of the same sex. It might involve simply an attraction that's confusing—a friendship that verges on the obsessive, for instance, or a married father of two who doesn't understand why he likes to trade e-mails with other men after midnight. This variation on the secret life of the homosexual might not even involve someone who is predominantly homosexual. Otherwise heterosexual persons are often threatened by an expression of homosexuality because it cuts too close to a part of themselves they don't like. If the response is to push back against this perceived threat, to forcibly distance the idea from themselves, it might take the form of gay jokes, cruelty, even hate crimes. Roy Cohn often went out of his way to say how much he hated homosexuals. A more accurate and honest expression of that sentiment, however, would have been an admission of how much he hated the homosexuality in himself.

Roy Cohn died of AIDS in 1986, when that epidemic was at its most vicious. In those days, one slogan in particular united AIDS activists. You would see it on buttons or flyers, or hear it chanted in the streets, especially in cities with large gay populations. This slogan was "Silence = Death"—meaning that if you didn't stand up to the forces of prejudice that interpreted "the gay plague" as a fitting punishment for an "evil" way of life, then you were complicit in the tragedy. But the equation can be equally poignant if read the other way and applied to the fate of Pyotr Ilyich Tchaikovsky. In 1892, according to some historians, a mock jury of his peers confronted him about his homosexuality and offered him the choice: exile to Siberia or death. They knew which he would choose. "Truly," Tchaikovsky had once declared, "there would be a reason to go mad if it were not for music." In Siberia, there would be no music. Four days later, at the age of fifty-three, Tchaikovsky was dead.

Because of his homosexuality, the world got to hear some of the most profound music ever composed, and because of his homosexuality, the world got to hear its absence—to learn what happens when, on a quite literal level, death equals silence.

[6 • THE SECRET LIFE OF THE PERVERSE]

Beat me, **** me, make me write bad checks.

—Popular graffito (c. 1980)

How did you get those scars?

I was whipped.

Where did this happen?

The Ottoman Empire.

When?

During the War.

Again:

How did you get those scars?

I was whipped.

Where did this happen?

Arabia.

When?

1917.

Again:

How did you get those scars?

I was whipped.

Where did this happen?

Deraa.

When?

The night of November 21 to 22, 1917.

Again.

And again. And again. And *again*. T. E. Lawrence began telling this story in 1919, and he continued telling it for years to come, until by the time he put it down in writing, in a private 1926 printing of his book *The Seven Pillars of Wisdom*, it had acquired such specificity of detail that to this day it remains the book's most famous passage:

> The corporal had run downstairs; and now came back with a whip of the Circassian sort, a thong of supple black hide, rounded, and tapering from the thickness of a thumb at the grip (which was wrapped in silver) down to a hard point finer than a pencil.
>
> He saw me shivering, partly, I think, with cold, and made it whistle over my ear, taunting me that before his

> tenth cut I would howl for mercy, and at the twentieth beg for the caresses of the Bey; and then he began to lash me madly across and across with all his might, while I locked my teeth to endure this thing which lapped itself like flaming wire about my body.

Lawrence went on to describe how he withstood the blows, counting them in order to keep his mind "in control," and experiencing the "gradual cracking apart" of his whole being. Finally, when he was completely broken, his tormentors

> seemed satisfied. Somehow I found myself off the bench, lying on my back on the dirty floor, where I snuggled myself, dazed, panting for breath, but vaguely comfortable. I had strung myself to learn all pain until I died, and no longer actor, but spectator, thought not to care how my body jerked and squealed. Yet I knew or imagined what passed about me.

"Knew or imagined" is a key distinction here. By the time of the book's publication, Thomas Edward Lawrence had long since attained the status of myth as the fearsome Lawrence of Arabia, conqueror of the Turks—a reputation he did everything to encourage. And he did, after all, always insist that the book was a fictional "memoir." But the depiction of his homosexual rape was so much more intense and startling than most of the other scenes that readers assumed that it was as factual as the rest of the book.

Then came *The Golden Warrior,* a 1990 biography that cited British war records placing T. E. Lawrence and another officer in Aqaba, four hundred miles from Deraa, on November 21 and 22, 1917.

So the most famous scene in the book was one that Lawrence might very well have imagined, or embellished, or at least altered to some extent. If the story was not one that Lawrence actually lived, or lived fully, or lived fully in one specific location over two particular days, it was clearly a tableau that he inhabited. It was, at the very least, what he *wished* he'd lived.

It was, in fact, we know now, what Lawrence *did* live, at various later points in his life. It was one he lived at "flagellation parties," where men gathered in closed rooms to whip one another into a state of ecstasy; it was one he lived with a manservant; it was one he lived again and again and again because he had no choice but to live it again and again and again. We now know that the great Lawrence of Arabia, the "no prisoners!" war hero and straight-backed, poised-on-a-camel's-hump icon of an all-conquering British Empire upon which the sun never set, was a pervert.

Pervert? That's a loaded word, and maybe a surprising one, but it's being used here for a reason. It's come to carry a judgmental meaning that, at least in the mental-health professions, it originally didn't and still doesn't have. For all its creakiness as a word, *perversion* still suggests an overturning of the norm, and the use of the word still reinforces the idea that a perversion is a radical departure from a part of sexuality that's common to everyone.

That part is aggression. It doesn't have to be the primary component of a person's sexual identity or of a specific sexual encounter. But aggression is a necessary component, because even as sex demands cooperation, it also requires conflict.

Aggression exists on a continuum; no person actually occupies either extreme. No one is purely passive or totally aggressive. As a prominent psychoanalyst has written about aggression in sexuality, "It is often a whisper, not a roar, and only a part, not the whole." It is always, however, a presence. And aggression in sex has a specific name: sadomasochism.

This idea might seem completely backward at first, a 180-degree turn from tenderness. How can an act of love, something we call "lovemaking," also be an act of aggression, of me-versus-you? Aggression, despite its common associations, doesn't have to imply putting emotional distance between one person and another. Even in the most loving sexual encounter, aggression and its dual elements of sadism and masochism do in fact add to the feeling of tenderness.

This is because, at the most basic level, sex is about the crossing of the so-called body boundary. It's all about getting one person's protrusions into the other person's openings, and even when this is done by mutual and vigorous consent, it's still a literal violation. The body experiences the object (penis, nipples, fingers, mouth, etc.) as alien, and decides whether it likes it or not. Maybe it enjoys these sensations, or maybe it experiences tension and resistance, a closing up of all doorways. Maybe it incorporates resistance, then yields, as an enhancement to sexual excitement.

People have sometimes commented that during sex they forget whose body is whose. This makes sense. Out of mutual dependence emerges, if only briefly, one independent being. Masculine, feminine, aggressor, aggressed, penetrator, penetrated, sadist, masochist: All the labels that have gotten the lovers to this single point suddenly melt away at the very height of erotic passion. Shakespeare's famous "beast with two backs" becomes, really, a beast with *one* back.

This, then, is bliss, or at least a pretty good approximation. It might be easy to imagine how such a state would become the focus of any lover's desires. The levels that sexual partners reach, and the variations of aggression they enact in order to reach those states, don't have to be conscious. In fact, each day millions of couples go to bed together without giving a single thought to the aggressive behaviors they enact while in the throes of intimacy.

But if a couple *does* give their behavior a thought, then they might become aware of the degree of aggression involved, and alter their sexual activities somewhat, to suit the mood. They might incorporate light bondage into their sex life—trying one's partner to the bedpost, or wearing a blindfold, or getting spanked. For these people, the voice of aggression might be somewhat louder than a "whisper."

It might be a voice they consciously hear, and it might be one they willingly listen to. But it also might be one they can choose to ignore. It's their choice.

Not so for those with a perversion. To be sure, that voice might not be the *only* sound they hear. People who need to be whipped all the time in order to feel pleasure, or who must be sadistic with others, or masturbate against stuffed animals, or have sexual intercourse with real animals, or who are aroused by children, or must expose their genitals to strangers, or any other perversion—such people can often in fact engage in "normal" sex. They might even perform as well as anyone else, and seem to their sexual partners to be perfectly "good in bed." But their secret life revolves around the fact that "normal" sex doesn't ever engage *them*. Such sex is like the tiniest flicker compared with the enormous flame that is their perversion. For them, "normal" sex is never the "roar."

Toby, age twenty-six, liked shoes. In fact, he always went with his girlfriends to Barneys or Bloomingdale's to help them pick out their shoes. His choices were always right, and his girlfriends, and then their friends, tended to regard him as some sort of metrosexual hero. Most men, after all, complain about being dragged into stores by women, yet Toby was not only willing and eager, but expert. He knew a good pair of Jimmy Choos when he saw one.

His new girlfriend, Kate, though, understood early on that Toby's interest in women's shoes went beyond style concerns and helpfulness. Once in a while, Toby convinced her to dress up in her "highest, dirtiest pair of shoes" and nothing else, and then have sex with him. Kate told him it reminded her of the *Sex and the City* episode in which the character of Charlotte goes into a shoe store and covets a pair of expensive shoes. The salesman agrees to give her the shoes for free in exchange for letting him rub and touch her feet. The more she lets him rub, the more shoes she gets for free. Toby had laughed along with Kate when she recounted the plot. But something was different about Toby, and he knew it. He could see Kate's look of wariness, feel her reservations, and as a result, the high-heeled sex with her wasn't as satisfying as he felt it could be. After a while, he stopped making the request, and that was that: no more shoe fantasies with Kate.

But shoe fantasies on his own? Toby didn't exactly indulge them. He wasn't a "pervert," after all. But, yes, he had thought about shoes. Stilettos, to be precise. Their sharpness. Those heels could be a weapon; they could stop a man in his tracks. But they could also hobble the person who wore them. They could render her as submissive as a Chinese woman with bound feet. In fact, Toby had fantasized about shoes and girls' feet since he was about thirteen. He and his younger sister would occasionally play a game in which she would put on her mother's high heels and walk on Toby's back until he would call out some form of "uncle." It was a contest of sorts to see who was tougher. Sometimes his sister won, and other times he did.

They'd always had an intense relationship. She was blond and sarcastic and fascinating, and when they were younger they would take naps together, and he remembered the unbelievable pleasure of his sister's head against his shoulder, her breaths coming softly against his neck, each one making him churn inside with a strange, overstimulated sensation. The household had crackled with excitement: pillow fights, getting undressed together to go swimming, secret trips to the kitchen together in the middle of the night. Their mother knew about the intensity between brother and sister and was amused by it; she herself was blond and powerful, and would let Toby light her cigarettes sometimes, which she smoked in one of those cool-looking holders, like Natasha from *Rocky and Bullwinkle*. The femaleness in the house was as palpable as a scent, and Toby couldn't get enough of it. As a grown man, he realized that his early memories had built up in power and clarity and gathered into a kind of ball over time, resulting in a tremendous excitement that was both indescribably thrilling and yet shameful, too. He saw his sister, his mother, a pair of shoes. He remembered being walked on, and the shape of those shoes, the awe they inspired in him, the helpless ecstasy.

One weekend when Kate was away visiting her sister, Toby took a pair of her shoes out of the closet. He'd had a couple of beers, he later told me; he felt loose and uninhibited. And then pretty soon he was lying in bed with one of those shoes rubbing against his groin. He ejaculated into the shoe far more quickly than he would have liked, and then spent the rest of the evening sheepishly trying to remove stains from the black leather.

But he couldn't deny it: The experience had been exciting, the sensations exquisite. He couldn't stop thinking about that night. It was as though the shoe had been waiting to be picked up and used in this specific way. He'd just been slow to see the possibilities. Why even go back to ordinary sex; it was tedious, *vanilla*. Shoes: He visualized them while sitting in his desk chair at work, while riding the subway, while lying in bed in the dark, Kate, untouched, beside him: their shape, their arch, the gaping mouth of an empty shoe just waiting to be filled by a woman's foot, by his own penis.

The roar inside Toby's head must have been very loud. But then, the roar inside the head of those living the secret life of the perverse is always deafening. For that very reason, it is also defining. The roar is all they hear, and the roar is all they are.

The roar is metaphorical; those "hearing" it don't have to clap their hands over their ears to drown it out. But in a manner of speaking, that's just what they do. The aggression they embody is so extreme that it feels as if, unleashed, it could devour anyone who gets in its path (and very occasionally it literally does, as was the case with the fictional character of Hannibal "the Cannibal" Lecter in the 1991 movie *The Silence of the Lambs*, and as has been the case for certain real-life serial killers such as Jeffrey Dahmer). The secret life of the perverse is all aggression, all the time.

And it therefore requires all control, all the time. The perverse spend their lives constructing the most elaborate controls possible out of whatever's available, like a bamboo cage for King Kong, or an ingenious modern steel-and-glass cell for Hannibal Lecter. (Is it any coincidence that Lecter's prison "uniform," complete with leather-and-metal mask and manacles, looked a lot like an outfit from an S&M boutique?) The perversion is not an aspect of a person's existence, part of his or her sexual repertoire, a little spice to share with an adventurous partner. The perversion is a need. It's consuming. It is "a central preoccupation of the person's existence," in the words of one psychoanalyst who has written on the topic. The perversion is what the perverse must do, it's what they must do soon, it's what they must do again and again, and it's what they must do in precisely one specific fashion. Not to do so is not an option.

The perverse tend to think that they exist outside the boundaries of "normal" society—and they do. Unlike the repetitive, compulsive actions of a chronic hand washer, which serve the supposed purpose of righting a wrong, a perversion serves the supposed purpose of *being* a wrong. But it's the repetitive nature of the behavior—the need to do the same thing in the same way again and again—that gives the lie to the lawlessness of the perverse. Even as they are trying to cage their aggression, the perversion is imprisoning them.

In a 2004 memoir called *The Surrender,* Toni Bentley, a former dancer with the New York City Ballet, detailed her long involvement and fascination with anal sex. Throughout the book, Bentley is admirably honest. She allows that in being anally penetrated she was trying to free herself from psychological constraints that began in childhood with a demanding father and continued throughout the decades of extraordinary physical punishment that becoming a world-class dancer requires. But how free is she? When she enters into a relationship with someone she calls only "A-Man," they never go anywhere or do much of anything, other than engage in sodomy, after which she saves the used condoms and totes up the number of times she's been anally penetrated. For all her supposed hedonism, she still has to contain—literally place inside a box—the results of her aggression.

In a way, a perversion is the opposite of intimacy. It's not that Toby, for instance, couldn't continue having sex with Kate. He did. It's just that sex with his living, breathing girlfriend had become meaningless for him. Not surprisingly, they broke up not long after Toby's first encounter with a shoe. Kate had complained to him that while she'd always noticed some emotional distance during their lovemaking, she'd always hoped it would get better, and they would grow closer. But lately, she said, during their most intimate moments Toby had always seemed to be "somewhere else." Which he was.

For the perverse, a sexual partner is not someone to open up to, not someone to share innermost secrets with. It's someone to control so that secrets *don't* spill out. Or, more accurately, it's not so much someone to control as some*thing* to control. It's an object that can be trusted do the same thing again and again in precisely the same fashion.

The most famous literary example of perversion can be found in Vladimir Nabokov's novel *Lolita*, which accurately captures the perils of injecting human nature into a perverse relationship. At the beginning of the story, the weary middle-aged college professor and pedophile Humbert Humbert (his name itself suggesting a double identity, as several generations of literary critics have noted) goes looking for a place to live. So besotted does he become by a prepubescent girl on his rounds of searching for available real estate that he rents a room in her mother's house. After the older woman's death in a car accident, he takes Lolita on a meandering road trip across America, the better to have her all to himself.

This, too, is bliss—or at least it is to Humbert Humbert, or at least he believes it is, for as long as it lasts. But then Lolita does the unthinkable: She gets older. She graduates from prepubescent to pubescent. She becomes an adult. She becomes *human*: impatient with his constant attentions, bored with their repetitiveness. And so she slips out of Humbert Humbert's control—and to lose control of the object is intolerable to the perverse. Time passes, as (sigh) it always does, and when at last Humbert locates Lolita again, she has fallen in love, gotten married, and is pregnant. *How dare she?*

Better, perhaps, to find a partner who is dependable, predictable, yet inanimate. (This train of thought doesn't necessarily lead to necrophilia, though in some extreme cases it might.) Though the perverse are able to turn other people into objects, just the way God turned Lot's wife into a pillar of salt, sometimes they choose to reject human partners altogether. They reroute the aggression away from some person and toward some *thing* that fits the specific requirements. This thing is what we call a fetish.

For Toby, it was the shoe. For T. E. Lawrence, it was the whip. In *Seven Pillars,* when Lawrence describes the whip that (supposedly) ripped his hide on November 21 to 22, 1917, he does so in rather extraordinary detail, considering that it was an object he must have been cowering from rather than studying for future discussion. It was, he wrote, "a whip of the Circassian sort, a thong of supple black hide, rounded, and tapering from the thickness of a thumb at the grip (which was wrapped in silver) down to a hard point finer than a pencil." He goes on to recount how the whip's lashings generated a "delicious warmth, probably sexual" swelling through him, and the way the corporal "flung up his arm and hacked with the full length of his whip into my groin."

For the fetishist in particular, on a literal level, and for the perverse in general, on a psychological level, the perversion is a replacement for sex. From all indications, Lawrence never once entered into an intimate relationship in his life. It has been theorized that he was a secret homosexual, but his friend Vyvyan Richards (who was unrequitedly in love with him) wrote that Lawrence possessed no "carnality" whatsoever. Lawrence himself wrote that he couldn't ever bring himself to have sex with other men. Regarding sex with women, Lawrence admitted that he had never engaged in it, nor did he very much want to. The impulse to touch another creature, he wrote, didn't exist in him.

If perversions are a parody of lawlessness and even, perhaps, a parody of sex itself, then the question arises: For whose benefit are the parodies being performed?

Sometimes the audience is literally present. Susannah, a woman who'd been singing lead with a rock band, had been on the road for years. The band was always on the verge of a breakthrough, but had never been able to go the distance. They played small, noisy clubs in various cities, and though not quite famous, they had made a name for themselves. In particular, Susannah had made a name for herself. She was from the Courtney Love school of female singers: loud, messy, vulgar, attention grabbing. Sometimes a young male fan would wait at the stage door after a show and chat her up, hoping he'd get a chance to go out with her. Once in a while, if the man was attractive, she would go off with him. But these were never "dates." Instead, Susannah liked to have sex with the man in a nearby location: often in the band's bus, which afforded its passengers no privacy whatsoever. The other band members would try to pretend they couldn't hear or see the couple going at it in the last row of seats, though given the proximity and the acoustics, it was difficult to miss, and Susannah knew it.

That was the point. Once in a while, one of the band members would tell her to "get a room," but Susannah knew she never would.

For her, the public nature of this kind of sex was a great part of its excitement. The idea of going to a motel room somewhere with a stranger seemed really unappealing. No, worse than unappealing: It seemed wrong. The kind of sex that she liked—fast, furious, anonymous, loud—was exciting only out in the open, in front of as many people as possible. It was just like being up onstage, grabbing the microphone and screaming out lyrics about love, only better.

Exhibitionism is a perversion in which the consuming fantasy that needs to be acted out is one in which you show your body. The "show" might consist of your sexual organs alone, or it might be your sexual organs engaged in sex. Either way, it's a *show*. It's not something being shared with a present, active participant. It's something being bestowed upon an imaginary passive audience. Without those onlookers, sex is meaningless, as was the case with Susannah.

Even if an audience isn't literally present, one still needs it to exist, if only in the imagination, in order for a perverse act to have meaning. Perhaps the most revealing phrase in T. E. Lawrence's written account of his rape had nothing to do with the whip and the pain. It was instead his description of himself at the key moment: "I had strung myself to learn all pain until I died, and *no longer actor, but spectator,* thought not to care how my body jerked and squealed" (emphasis added).

Homosexual rape was hardly a fit subject for conversation in Great Britain in the 1920s, but Lawrence made sure to include his experience of it, in loving detail. He wanted readers to see what he saw: a man bent, breaking. More to the point, he wanted himself to see what he saw—wanted himself to believe the image he was conjuring up before his very eyes. For Lawrence, all the world actually *was* his stage.

The performance in a perverse act is always an act of deception. On the surface, the fantasy might seem to reveal a brazen nature. But in fact it has been unconsciously designed to conceal a deeper truth. The overt message of the exhibitionist is: "Look at my genitals; aren't they amazing?" The hidden meaning of the exhibitionist is: "I fear my genitals are damaged, worthless, nothing." The overt message of the voyeur is: "I like to watch; I'm a passive presence." The hidden meaning is: "I want to invade this scene; I want to be doing that, and that, and *that*."

The overt message of the perverse is: "I crave consummation." The hidden—the *secret*—meaning is: "I can't handle intimacy." And as the perversion comes to dominate a life, so does the performance, so does the deception, and so does the inability to achieve intimacy—not only with a sexual partner, but with anyone.

Deception would have come easily to Lawrence. At an early age he learned that his parents were not who they appeared to be. His father had once been called Thomas Chapman, and his mother, Sarah, had been employed as the governess of Thomas Chapman's daughters—his children by another woman, his first wife. The new couple, Thomas and Sarah, living in social disgrace, took the surname Lawrence and had five sons, the second one being Thomas Edward.

In changing their name, the newly minted Lawrences attempted to change the truth about themselves. Their son, over time, would try to alter perceptions of himself as well. So what, exactly, was he so desperately trying to disguise? For T. E. Lawrence, the source of the deep and irresolvable conflict over aggression may well have been his relationship with his mother. She was cruel, and she beat him regularly on the buttocks. Lawrence, on the other hand, was strongly willful. And so, on a regular basis, the irresistible force met the immovable object. The more he resisted her authority, the more she beat him, and vice versa. Psychologically speaking, what such behavior on her part would communicate to a son was more than punishment. It was ownership: *I possess you, and I can control your volatile emotions through the manipulation of pain*. A boy whose mother owns him can never become melded emotionally with her. And it's fair to say that such a boy may well grow up to be a man who cannot meld emotionally with women, or, if he's gay, with other men. Such a man might use his feelings of impotent rage to rebel against authority—in Lawrence's case, to become the leader of an underdog revolt. And then this stance might well become sexualized, ending, as it did for Lawrence, with fantasies of rape, and with rape itself. Such a man stays emotionally separate from other people—whether above them or below them, or banishing them altogether.

Lawrence, a military man, responded to the idea of "rigor"; a certain asceticism influenced numerous aspects of his life. He often followed his successes with bouts of self-denial, as if to negate his accomplishments. In late October 1918, less than two weeks before the armistice that ended the Great War, he appeared before King George V to receive two of the highest honors of the empire, yet he refused them at the last possible moment. The astonished king remarked that he was left "holding the box in my hand."

Did Lawrence pursue his perversion to the ends of the earth, or did it pursue him? As it came to dominate his life, his attempt at self-negation eventually took a more extreme form: self-erasure. In August 1922, he adopted the name John Hume Ross and enlisted in the Royal Air Force. When a newspaper discovered his secret identity four months later, he had no choice but to return to civilian life. He remained T. E. Lawrence, however, only briefly. In March 1923, he disappeared again, this time adopting the name T. E. Shaw and joining the Royal Tank Corps. He persuaded a companion to join him in the military, one John Bruce, whose role it was to gather birch branches on a regular basis and then whip "Shaw." Why? Because "Shaw" had behaved badly, according to numerous "letters" supposedly written by a close relation of his. "Shaw" clearly deserved to be punished, and "Shaw" was willing to accept his punishment. "Thanks," Lawrence would tell Bruce at the end of an evening's flagellation. "Good job."

Unlike Charles Lindbergh, T. E. Lawrence didn't adopt an alias in one smugly satisfying area of his life yet remain a heroic figure to the world at large. He actually attempted to *remove* Lawrence of Arabia from the world. To some extent, he succeeded on his second try; in 1927, four years after informally adopting the name of T. E. Shaw, he had his name changed legally.

But nobody could mistake Lawrence for a man of humility or passivity. He published an extensive account of his exploits, and in that book he openly reveled in the cruelties of combat—cruelties that easily might have exceeded the needs of the situation. "Blood was always on our hands: we were licensed to it," he wrote in the opening chapter of *Seven Pillars*.

> Wounding and killing seemed ephemeral pains, so very brief and sore was life with us. With the sorrow of living so great, the sorrow of punishment had to be pitiless. We lived for the day and died for it. When there was reason and desire to punish we wrote our lesson with gun or whip immediately in the sullen flesh of the sufferer, and the case was beyond appeal. The desert did not afford the refined slow penalties of courts and gaols.

You don't have to read between the lines to see who Lawrence was. These *are* the lines, for all the world to see. The sadistic figure of boundless aggression is who T. E. Lawrence most feared he was, and the masochistic figure of powerlessness—the whipping boy deserving of the whip—is how he most wanted to see himself.

"He is such an *infernal* liar!" Mrs. George Bernard Shaw once exclaimed of her good friend T. E. Lawrence. Her husband (presumably the inspiration for the surname that Lawrence eventually legally adopted), however, saw their friend differently: "He was not a liar. He was an actor."

Lawrence himself put it best. "History isn't made of truth, anyhow, so why worry?" he would say. "On the whole I prefer lies to truth, particularly where they concern me." People, however, tend to want the truth about other people, not lies. People want answers. They want to know other people's secrets. They want intimacy. Which is why the perverse prefer objectified people, or objects themselves. Objects don't want to know secrets, don't crave intimacy. They just sit there and take what's coming to them.

[7 • THE SECRET LIFE OF THE ADDICT]

Hi, my name is ______, and I am an alcoholic.

—Millions of recovering alcoholics worldwide

Stuart had grown up knowing that one day he would inherit the family sporting-goods business from his father, and Stuart's son had grown up knowing that one day he would inherit the family business from Stuart, and that's what made it a family business. And when the day came that Stuart had to hand over the daily operations of the family business to his son, he did so before two dozen of the company's employees, in the reception area of the front office on the Avenue of the Americas in Manhattan, above what was by then the flagship store. Then he had added, "Of course, I'm not going anywhere. You'll have to carry me out of here in a box."

Everybody laughed. Everybody knew that Stuart *was* Stuart's Sporting Goods, even if the Stuart in the company name had been his father. The business that had begun in a single store on Atlantic Avenue in Brooklyn back in the 1930s had expanded since Stuart took over in the 1950s into a sixteen-outlet empire that stretched across the tristate area. Along the way, he had personally approved every line of the company's advertising copy in local newspapers and on radio and television. Stuart had personally made the overseas trips to seal deals with wholesalers in Taiwan, Düsseldorf, and Leningrad when it was still Leningrad. Stuart had personally scouted locations, planted symbolic shovels in dirt, paid off politicians and mobsters.

And now it was his son's turn to be Stuart's Sporting Goods, which was all well and good, and as it should be. Stuart settled into an office down the hall from the corner office he'd occupied for nearly forty years, and he was allowed to keep his secretary, and sometimes his son asked him for advice. But the change was unmistakable. For the first time in his life, Stuart felt expendable. He began arriving later, leaving earlier, taking longer lunches. In the old days, he'd made it a rule never to have a drink at lunch; he didn't want to lose his competitive edge, as he always said. But now, he figured, what was the harm? So he would order a gin and tonic, and when he got back to the office the world was a little fuzzy and he was a little sleepy, and not long after he'd returned from lunch, Stuart would go home.

The cocktail hour had always started at six, but now that he was home earlier, he would fix himself a drink at five, and one for his wife, and the two of them would sit in the library by the window with a view of the East River, a bowl of nuts between them, and discuss the day. After a while Stuart would ask if his wife wanted her drink freshened, and she would decline, but Stuart would fix himself another, and eventually a servant would announce dinner, which was always accompanied by wine. By eight most evenings, Stuart couldn't keep his eyes open.

Stuart noticed that he was drinking more, but the fact was, the midday gin and tonic eased the sting of returning to an empty desk. Before long, he found that two gin and tonics eased the sting even more. By the end of his first year in retirement, Stuart was up to three gin and tonics, and most days after lunch he didn't even bother going back to the office anymore. Cocktail hour now started whenever Stuart got home.

He kept up appearances, or thought he did, anyway. True, his face was turning splotchy, but this discoloration could have been the effects of aging. And sometimes he thought he saw a waiter or the doorman looking at him a little too carefully, as if he might be walking unsteadily, which, to be honest, he sometimes was. "Let them look," was his attitude. For that matter, let his son sigh at the office, his wife tsk-tsk at the dinner table, his daughter-in-law hesitate on the phone when he'd suggest that he babysit his granddaughter. He'd worked hard every day of his life since the age of fifteen; he'd earned the right to enjoy himself a little too much once in a while. If not now, when?

"Are *you* going to be Stuart's Sporting Goods one day?" he whispered to his two-year-old granddaughter, Stacy, late one rainy Saturday afternoon, standing over her in the guest bedroom. Stuart had been playing with her ever since her parents had dropped her off that morning, on their way to an upstate wedding, and now he'd finally convinced her to take a nap. She had just fallen asleep, curled under a crocheted quilt. Stuart let himself out of the room, walked down the hall to the library, and poured himself a drink. It was his first of the day; he'd abstained so far because his wife was out at an all-day benefit auction, and he wanted to stay sharp while attending to his granddaughter. But now Stacy was asleep, and surely after playing Chutes and Ladders for two hours straight he deserved some kind of reward. He made his drink a double, settled into his favorite wingback chair by the window overlooking the river, and took a sip.

That evening he was awakened by the shouts of his daughter-in-law. It took him a moment to remember where he was, and then another moment to realize why his daughter-in-law would be there, and then a further moment to recognize what her shouts meant. She was shouting at him—at Stuart. She was saying something about coming back to the apartment and finding Stacy in the middle of the bed, in a diaper that had leaked through, in the dark, crying. *"How could you do this?"* she was saying, and then she said it again and again. *"How could you do this to Stacy? How could you do this to me, your daughter-in-law?"*

And then, dry-eyed and straightbacked with a suddenness that for some reason frightened Stuart, she said, "How could you do this to yourself?"

Alcoholics Anonymous was founded on a spring evening—Mother's Day, to be precise—in 1935 in Akron, Ohio. A visiting New York stockbroker who had recently given up drinking, Bill Wilson, was enlisted by an acquaintance to try to help a local surgeon whose own drinking had led to his dismissal from the city hospital and was now threatening to end his private practice. Wilson arrived at the home of the surgeon at 5 P.M., expecting to deliver a brief pep talk. Instead, the two men talked until eleven. Wilson had recently been declaiming about the evils of drink with an evangelical zeal, but on this evening he reversed his way of thinking about his whole approach. Rather than say that he was there to help, Wilson found himself confessing to the surgeon that *he* was the one in need of help. "You see, our talk was a completely mutual thing," Wilson later wrote. "I had quit preaching. I knew that I needed this alcoholic as much as he needed me. *This was it.*"

By the early 1950s, Alcoholics Anonymous counted one hundred thousand recovering alcoholics in the United States. Today AA counts a hundred thousand *chapters* around the world. Almost from the start the organization had spawned two natural extensions of its concept: Al-Anon, for the family members of alcoholics, and Narcotics Anonymous, for drug abusers. But over the decades, AA has also licensed the 12-step model more than six hundred times, and today the "Anonymous" label covers shoplifters, debtors, cancer patients, victims of domestic violence, sufferers from attention deficit disorder and depression, and even blocked artists.

Not all these groups deal with addictions, of course. Many merely borrow the 12-step model, and some only the "Anonymous" concept. Still, the sheer numbers give some sense of how pervasive is the concept of support groups. The era of addicts not having support groups seems as remote today as does, well, Mother's Day in Akron, Ohio, in 1935.

Even today, a stigma clings. The desire to remain anonymous is itself an indication that society isn't entirely accepting of addictions, even among addicts who admit they have a problem and are seeking help. However much society might agree that addiction is an illness, it is also often and widely interpreted, perhaps unwittingly, as a moral or emotional weakness. To be dependent or vulnerable or lacking in self-discipline are negative attributes in our society. Showing up with the shakes for a 9 A.M. meeting can get you sent to human resources—or get you fired.

Compounding the problem is the addict's own sense of shame. Whether society's attitude toward and interpretations of addiction are medically sound is almost irrelevant when it comes to how addicts view themselves, either before or after they accept the addiction as a fact of their lives. The judgment that society passes on an individual is the one that the individual tends to accept as well, at least on some level; witness the inner turmoil of some homosexuals who might otherwise be perfectly accepting of their own sexual preference.

For both these reasons—outside disapproval and inner shame—addicts by nature are veteran secret-keepers. As is always the case in a secret life, addicts work hard to keep their secret from the rest of the world. But as is usually *not* the case in a secret life, addicts also work hard to keep the secret of their addiction from themselves.

They do this through denial. Many addicts simply can't admit that that's what they are. That's why the first of the twelve steps in the Alcoholics Anonymous recovery program is an admission of alcoholism.

Part of the problem in reaching this first step is that the line between a heavy drinker and an alcoholic—in general, between a person with a bad habit and a substance abuser—isn't always clear. If the use of a substance is rendering someone unable to function at work, school, *or* home, then that person has an abuse problem. Holding down responsibilities on the job but falling apart at home? That qualifies as substance abuse. Performing admirably at home but blowing deadlines at work? That qualifies, too. Continuing to use the substance even after problems have arisen—in Stuart's case, even after he picked up disapproving cues from a doorman, a waiter, his wife, son, and daughter-in-law? That qualifies, and then some.

Even in the face of such evidence, addicts will still find powerful motivations to deny their addiction to themselves. After all, it's pleasant in here—in the realm of the eternal buzz. There's the invincibility of the cocaine high, the pulsing, drumming blood rush, the sense of never having been so aware, so alive. There's the languid liquidity of heroin, an initial pleasure bordering on ecstasy, followed by hours of luxuriously foggy detachment. There's the conviviality of alcohol, the loosening of the tongue and lowering of inhibitions, the illusion of eloquence and courage.

The addictive agent in question doesn't even have to be a literal substance. All it has to do is lead to an alteration of the state of consciousness. The high emotional stakes in gambling can create their own brain-chemistry-scrambling cycle of rewards, regardless of the actual monetary amounts, and even when the house is winning big.

Besides, the various paths to addiction are (mostly) legal. Alcohol is. Illegal drugs are, by definition, not, and therefore carry a higher level of social opprobrium, though even then they're tolerated or winked at in some circles—for example, cocaine in Hollywood or steroids in sports. And gambling? Entire cities are built around it. State treasuries have become as dependent on revenue streams from lottery sales as have the individual bettors who support the government's fiscal habit. Society's message to an addict is not only potentially hypocritical but enabling: "We condone this; you're just having fun like everyone else; just know when enough's enough."

To an addict, though, enough is never enough. Instead, too much is just about right.

• • •

When Abby lived in Manhattan, she used to meet up with the same group of friends several nights a week, first for dinner, then for a round of barhopping. They were young and resilient and worked out regularly; Abby could be back at her desk in the publicity department of a major publishing house in midtown by 10 a.m., none the worse for wear.

Nobody in Abby's group was counting the ticks on a biological clock yet; nobody was looking to find a man and settle down. But who could argue with falling in love? And so Abby was the first in her group to get married, the first to have a baby, the first to leave the city. It had been Kevin's idea to leave the city—easy for him to say, because he still got to go there every day for work. But Abby was holed up 24/7 in the "Bermuda Triangle" known as Kingswood, New Jersey. So Abby arranged that every Wednesday her mother-in-law, who lived three towns over, would visit and babysit Chloe, and Abby would take the train into Manhattan and meet with her friends. But it wasn't the same. The fun now started at noon, with lunch not dinner, and Abby would have to listen to her friends talk about the clubs they'd been to, the promotions they were getting. Eventually someone would ask politely about her life, but what could she say: *"Chloe had a long nap yesterday so last night was hell"*? Or maybe: "*Chloe just hates broccoli"*? Besides, buzzed or not, everybody but Abby needed to be back at their desks by a respectable time. Sometimes Abby got a friend to agree to "play hooky," and together the two of them would go off to a wine bar until the afternoon had melted away. But usually Abby lingered alone, sometimes shopping a little, or maybe catching a movie, but always stopping for a drink on her way back to Penn Station. On the ride home, she'd think about how she would soon be spending the evening changing diapers and humming lullabies while her friends would be picking up where they'd left off at lunch. So she would, too. As soon as she could hustle her mother-in-law out the door, Abby would reach into the refrigerator for the remnants of last night's bottle of white wine.

And not just on Wednesdays. By the time Chloe hit the terrible twos, Abby had perfected the routine of plunking her in a stroller and making the quarter-mile walk to Parson's Wines and Liquors. Once inside the store, with its corky smell and kind old salesman, Abby would grab a few bottles and bring them up to the counter. Then she would make the return walk home and plop Chloe in front of the TV. There was nothing wrong with letting kids watch TV. Caillou and Barney and Dora the Explorer became Chloe's best friends. Chardonnay became Abby's.

Abby consciously calculated how to keep her drinking secret. She learned to smile sweetly at the clerk at Parson's, discourage her mother-in-law's unannounced visits, drive the empties to the dump before her husband got home. But she had also unconsciously calculated how to deny the reality to herself. She told herself that she was only doing what she used to do when she lived in the city; that she was only doing what her friends were still doing; that she was only doing what she herself would be doing, if she were somehow childless again, and single, and sharing the rent on a two-bedroom apartment in the East Seventies. What she didn't tell herself was that her level of alcohol consumption had passed the point of no return—no return, that is, except to admit that she was an alcoholic. When a friend would call and Abby would have to work overtime not to slur her words, or when her husband would come home in the evening and curl his lip and pronounce the house a disaster area, Abby certainly knew she was drunk. She just wasn't *a drunk*.

Denial is always a powerful psychological force, but in the case of the addict, it can be further reinforced by a physiological component. It doesn't take long for the body to adjust to new levels of chemicals, whether they've been introduced from the outside or rechoreographed from the inside. All drugs of abuse affect the brain's flow of dopamine, a chemical messenger that often communicates pleasure through motivation and reward. Cocaine, for instance, interferes with the flow of dopamine, causing it to build up and stimulate the same neurons again and again; as a result, the user experiences a sense of euphoria. But the high will last only about half an hour, and users who have been ingesting cocaine regularly report that they need greater and greater amounts to achieve the same high.

And just as the addictive substance in question doesn't even have to be a literal substance to lead to an alteration of the state of consciousness, so it doesn't have to introduce new chemicals into the body. All it has to do is lead to an alteration of the brain's chemistry. Magnetic resonance imaging (MRI) has shown, as one neuroscientist reported, "that a monetary reward in a gambling-like experiment produces brain activation very similar to that observed in a cocaine addict receiving an infusion of cocaine."

Whatever its source, the high comes to require more and more maintenance: more of the substance or experience, and more often. And as the craving takes over, an addict's already chemically and neurologically impaired judgment becomes ever more unreliable, sometimes even ruinously so.

Maggie Rizer entered modeling the summer after she graduated from high school. Her mother had seen a segment on *Oprah* called "Can Your Child Be a Star?" and had sent a head shot of Maggie to the Ford Modeling Agency in New York City. Before long, the stunning blonde from working-class Watertown, New York, was earning thirty thousand dollars a day for photo shoots and twenty thousand per fashion show—and doing eighty of them a year. Then one day in early 2003, at the age of twenty-five, Maggie woke up broke. Her financial manager—who also happened to be her stepfather—had somehow managed to lose all of her seven million dollars in savings.

Maggie had hired him against her better judgment. When she'd come home one day and said she now had a financial planner to manage her newfound fortune, her stepfather said he was hurt. He asked why she should be giving 5 percent of her income to a stranger when he, a veteran of the insurance business, had always been smart about money. Maggie hesitated. "Don't mix business with family," she told herself. But after a sleepless night, she agreed.

At first he dutifully paid her bills, invested in mutual funds, behaved in a strictly professional manner. And then he discovered Quick Draw.

It was strictly legal, a state-run lottery game. But as its name hints, it involved a certain degree of treachery, of sleight of hand. The game was commonly called "video crack," and for someone like John Breen, it was irresistible.

He'd already overcome one addiction, or thought he had, anyway. Alcohol had been his poison of choice, but as far as he knew, he'd put that problem behind him. Then he hit the jackpot: his stepdaughter's modeling career. Having hit one jackpot, however, only triggered the typical addict's response in Breen: Where's the next one? And so he set out to find it, every day down at the Speak Easy tavern. There he would sit all afternoon, sipping from the bottomless glass of vodka at his elbow, endlessly filling out Quick Draw tickets, fifty at a time, every five minutes. Even with a maximum bet of $10 per ticket, that kind of wagering could add up to $60,000 a week. But he had his stepdaughter's account to draw on—or borrow from, as he preferred to see the situation. Before long, he was writing checks he couldn't possibly cover, forging authorizations, closing out Maggie's retirement accounts early, all the while reassuring himself that he'd pay everything back once he hit it big.

"Hitting bottom," it's called. But, to coin a phrase, one man's floor is another man's ceiling. A life that to an outsider might seem to be spiraling furiously out of control might seem to the person actually living it to be manageable. Addicts routinely lose money, friends, home, family—everything—but the addiction still prevails. Sometimes what breaks the cycle is practical: Your supplier dries up, you run out of money. In that case, the impetus for change isn't so much a desire to improve yourself as it is an inability to maintain the addiction.

But sometimes the desire to change can come from within. That was the case with Stuart, the sporting-goods magnate. The Saturday evening his daughter-in-law had stood over him, berating him, he'd managed to pull himself out of his chair and walk out of the library to the foyer, where his son was holding Stacy tight. It wasn't his daughter-in-law's shouts that finally reached him, he later told me. It wasn't his son's look of disgust and anger. It was the terror on his granddaughter's face, the way she twisted away from him, burying herself deep in her father's shoulder. That's what made Stuart finally say to himself, "Something's wrong with me."

For an addict, that admission might well be the beginning of the end of the addiction. The secret of the addiction has now become not only public knowledge but private knowledge. The wall of denial has begun to crumble, and what rises in its place is the possibility of acceptance. But what made that wall so high and strong in the first place? Aside from the fact of the addiction, what is it that addicts fight so hard to deny? What have they got to hide from themselves? What is the secret behind the secret?

We think we know. Several studies of the most extreme cases of addiction have found one pattern again and again—even "invariably," in the surprisingly definitive language of one researcher.

At a key stage in life, children need to take the psychologically healthy step of learning to distinguish themselves from their parents. They need to develop a self-boundary—a dividing line that separates them from everything and everyone else not just bodily but emotionally and intellectually. But future addicts don't complete this step. Their efforts end in frustration. They are discouraged from learning that they can and do have thoughts that their parents don't and can't: thoughts that are, by definition, secrets; secrets that are, in turn, the key to the development of an individual identity. They fail to achieve separation.

How so? Maybe a parent discourages such thoughts of independence by telling the two-year-old that he or she doesn't "really" have secrets. All children believe that their parents can read their thoughts, but in this case, a child will *continue* to believe that the parent can read his or her thoughts. "What would Mommy think?" a child might wonder when a "bad" thought pops into his head. The healthy response: *Well, I'm just going to think my thought anyway, because it's my thought.* The child who is being thwarted in his or her quest for emotional independence, however, will feel that Mommy already knows about the "bad" thought—so he or she had better stop thinking it, pronto, and just stuff it way back deep down inside. *Secrets? What secrets? Who needs secrets?*

A narcissistic parent doesn't even have to suppress a child's secrets directly. Maybe a parent becomes jealous of a child's transitional object—a favorite stuffed animal, or even a real pet. The parent might regard the object as a rival for the child's affections rather than as a healthy helpmate for a child who is beginning to make his or her first forays into the big wide world, and needs to do so alone yet not alone. The child's message: *I need to go off exploring by myself—just me and my little stuffed animal.* The parent's response: *Can I go, too?*

Of course, not every child who fails to achieve a clear and separate sense of self becomes an addict. (And not every addict suffers from unfortunate parenting. In some cases, both the addiction and the resistance to overcoming it may be the result of a biological or genetic influence. Addictions sometimes do run in families.) But many addicts seem to share this psychological background. At the early age that future substance abusers first get the chance to separate from their parents by having "secret" thoughts and feelings, they find that the boundary between themselves and the rest of the world doesn't exist. And so they spend the rest of their lives trying to escape the feeling of being both suffocated *and* isolated—as if they'd been born in an overcrowded, stalled elevator and had spent their whole lives there. They know they want out, but they can't imagine how to get there.

Claire, twenty-six, had heard about studies that said some people are born shy, and that certainly seemed true of her. She couldn't remember a time when she didn't feel socially awkward, or when her face didn't redden if she was called on in class. But now she was starting work as a banker at a high-pressure investment firm, and she was afraid her shyness would get the best of her. At the company party on a chartered boat, she put on a pretty good show, talking to various people, but by the middle of the day she was almost shaking from the effort she'd put into everything, and the falseness she felt doing so.

So when she popped into the women's room and saw two other young bankers doing coke there, she was glad to partake. One line and she felt much better; she rejoined the group on the deck, and this time she found herself laughing and talking with ease. The coke reminded her of how much she'd liked the drug back in college, and she discreetly asked one of the other women where she might buy some. Within two days, Claire had her own stash, and she used it at first in situations where she needed to be extroverted. But as time passed, she used it whenever she felt like it. Coke made her feel that interactions were easy. To Claire, it was a lifesaver, and she made sure to have a gram stashed in her purse at all times.

At a company retreat, Claire stayed up late with four other employees, standing around the piano in the lounge off the lobby and singing old Beatles songs. She was in top form, she thought, outgoing and funny. She loved her coworkers, and she could have stayed there all night in the warmth of the fireplace and the brandy and the cocaine she'd discreetly inhaled.

But around 1 A.M., the other people began saying their good

nights. Claire protested, but they shook their heads and said they'd had enough. "Enough?" Claire called after them in a mock-joking fashion. "You don't know the meaning of *enough*!" Everybody laughed, then everybody left. As she stood in the lounge by herself Claire couldn't help but notice how deafening the silence was, in contrast to all the noise they'd been producing.

"*I've* been producing," she thought. Everybody at the retreat had been awkward at first; the whole point of a corporate retreat was to "get to know" your coworkers. But Claire was the one who needed to be the life of the party, who wanted to be everyone's friend. Now the votive candles were burning low on the ledges along the backs of the banquettes, and she saw that she was all alone.

This forlorn moment hints at the central paradox of the secret life of the addict. Left to their own devices, addicts find they don't *have* any of their own devices—or very few that would help them make their way in the world. Their earliest efforts at establishing inner resources were stymied; they tried, as children must, to develop a healthy self-boundary, and they failed. And so, having never secured a sense of "self," they've likewise never been able to establish a sense of "other," either. Instead, they inhabit a netherworld, a perpetual purgatory that is neither here nor there, and that leaves them feeling simultaneously smothered and bereft.

The buzz is what makes this existence bearable. The perpetual fuzziness can endow an addict with the courage to attempt to enter the outside world, and it can feed the illusion that the attempt was successful. It lowers inhibitions within, and it lifts the veil without. But this relationship with the outside world is based on a double deception. What addicts offer the outside world isn't a genuine inner self but an imitation—a counterfeit version that they can bear to part with. And what addicts believe they're getting in return is also an imitation—a version of the outside world that has been softened to the point that it has lost its threatening edge. Just as the secret life of the lover consists of a series of pseudo intimacies, so the secret life of the addict consists of a series of pseudo surrenders: one attempt after another to merge with the world, all doomed to failure.

When Claire returned to her hotel room the night of her cocaine binge at the company retreat, she stood before the bathroom mirror and examined her bloodshot eyes and blotchy complexion. "I look like crap," she thought. In the morning she looked in the mirror again, only this time it was the mirror of her compact, flat on the nightstand, its surface lined with two white streaks. What other choice did she have? The feeling of fellowship with her coworkers the night before might have been fleeting, even illusory, but at least it was a *feeling*. It was the closest connection with the outside world she had ever known.

A failure to find connection or completion or wholeness doesn't erase the craving for connection or completion or wholeness. If anything, the ongoing frustration only reinforces the primal frustration—the child's inability to separate properly from his or her parents, the failure to establish the crucial boundary between the self and the rest of the world that set this cycle in motion. This frustration—this failure to separate—is the secret at the center of their lives. This is the secret that first led to their addiction, and that ever since has fed their denial. And so, like Claire bending over the mirror of her compact, the addict returns to the scene of the crime, so to speak. The bottle, the needle, the taste or snort or endorphin rush are reenactments of the moment when that early trauma first embedded itself in his or her unconscious. Having been frustrated at a formative stage of development—having been forbidden from forming an identity—addicts now reveal and reveal and reveal out of fear they've got nothing to say, no self to surrender. The alcoholic at the corner tap telling his life story to the apathetic bartender might be a stereotype, but it's one grounded in as much psychological reality as the coke addict who won't shut up. But at the end of the day, as with Claire in the piano lounge alone, the connection with the outside world proves illusory—the outside world that for the addict is always too much, yet never enough.

[8 • THE SECRET LIFE OF THE CRIMINAL]

Steal this book.

—Abbie Hoffman (1971)

It started small: A pair of women's thermal socks at a sporting-goods store, dark green and not to her taste, but still she wanted them. She wanted them *idly*, as if they were one of those items located near the checkout counter that you suddenly decide to put into your cart "just because." This was impulse shoplifting, done without any real thought attached. After the socks there was a Hi-Liter pen that stood in a bouquet of identical pens on the counter of a stationery store. Diane simply plucked and pocketed it while the salesman was looking away.

As it turned out, Diane would never use that pen; she had nothing to highlight. She was long past her student days, her single days. At age fifty-one, she was married and the mother of three grown children who had all left home. She had reached that full-circle point in life, in fact, where it was now her turn to take care of her elderly father, who had just been moved from his apartment to a nearby nursing home. Her life had otherwise slowed down over the past few years, as lives eventually tend to do. Her days were calm and predictable, and she was grateful for the empty-nest time she got to spend with her husband, a wry, quiet man who still made her laugh.

The suburb where Diane and Paul lived wasn't exactly exciting, but it met the needs of a middle-aged, middle-class couple. One of its central features was an enormous mall, which attracted people from the area like worshippers to Mecca. Even on the coldest days you could drive there, step inside, and feel warm and secure. You could linger for half the day, nursing a cappuccino at one of the many stands in the food court, and you could weave in and out of stores, buying or just looking.

Diane had never been an acquisitive person; her tidy ranch house wasn't one of those places where every surface was covered with knickknacks. Whenever a friend gave her a small, decorative gift, she would inwardly sigh, thinking, "Where am I supposed to put that?" Which is why it made no sense to her that she'd developed this increasingly irresistible habit of taking small items from stores and slipping them into her pocket or purse, then blithely gliding out the door. "Have a good day!" a salesgirl would sometimes call, and Diane would smile and wave good-bye, her other hand thrust into her own pocket or bag, cradling the stolen object.

No logical thought or deliberation ever went into the decision to lift any of the trivial things that, over a couple of months, began to add up: socks, pens, coffee mugs, magazines, lipstick in bright shades that she would never use. Growing up, she had known girls who from time to time had stolen lip gloss or small trinkets, but she seemed to recall that they had done so because they didn't have enough money to pay for those items. She also remembered that the things the girls stole were alluring and appealing to them, and that they'd spent a great deal of time making a decision about what to take before actually taking it—the way people mulled over a serious decision to buy something significant. Diane herself had been far too ethical ever to shoplift back then, preferring to save her babysitting money until she could afford what she really wanted.

But here, now, as a middle-aged woman, she didn't want the stuff she took. She just . . . took, for the sake of taking. She brought these oddly meaningless objects home, like Charles Foster Kane returning from a trip abroad, and put them in her own version of storage, a box in the back of the top shelf on her side of the bedroom closet. There they simply sat. No one knew about them—not her husband, Paul, or her father, or her best friend, to whom she usually confided everything. The items were just *there,* taking up space, gathering in number as time passed, a nonsensical grab bag of unwanted, yet somehow strangely wanted, items. Knowing they were there, and how they'd gotten there, gave her a feeling of, if not exactly pleasure, then something related to it. Comfort? Security? Excitement? Superiority? It was hard to pin the sensation down, and Diane didn't see the point in thinking about it anyway. Instead, she allowed herself simply to experience it: look, take, pocket, hide; look, take, pocket, hide.

Because none of the salespeople had ever seemed to regard her with the slightest suspicion, Diane became more relaxed and emboldened, moving from sundries like socks and pens to larger items such as expensive clothing, though even these were not things she coveted. Still, she forged ahead as though on a determined, secret mission, returning to the mall again and again, until it began to feel like an extension of home.

Diane's bout of shoplifting ended swiftly on the afternoon she left a clothing boutique and felt a hand on her shoulder. At first she assumed she was being approached by a friend, and she turned expectantly, only to find herself facing instead a bald, middle-aged man in a crisp gray uniform. Even then she found herself thinking, "What would he want with me?" It was as though Diane had never really taken seriously the idea that one day someone might actually see what she was doing and stop her.

"Ma'am?" he said.

Diane let her bag drop to the floor and began to cry softly. She wasn't really a shoplifter; surely he would see that. She was respectable. She had money. She didn't need to steal, and she certainly didn't need the dress that she'd pushed into her bag today. It was a size six, while she herself wore a ten. The whole thing would have been comical, if the guard's manner hadn't been so serious, his grip on her elbow so strong as he led her through the crowd that parted before the two of them, the faces of neighbors and strangers alike looking back at her skeptically, suspiciously, as if she were a criminal.

Criminal behavior is an umbrella term for any kind of activity that is in violation of the law. As a society, we construct laws to protect ourselves from those among us who not only feel the desire to steal or harm, but who act on that impulse. And the difference between the two—between the feeling and the action—is the difference between the jungle and civilization.

The impulse itself is human nature. We are an aggressive species. We feel the impulse to hit, to take, to grab, slap, shout, shove, shove back, and shove back some more. Standing on a subway platform at rush hour, the blaring static of the loudspeaker piercing your brain, the blown deadline at work pounding your temples, the heat and stink swelling the very air around you, immobilizing you, as you stare into a tunnel for the sign of light that just doesn't come, you might think: "I could push that old woman over there onto the tracks."

You don't push her, of course, though the thought of doing so—even the thought that you might be *capable* of doing so—could unsettle you. But as is always the case with fantasies, it would be a mistake to confuse thinking blasphemous thoughts with carrying them out. We are always approaching and retreating from transgression, meeting crimes in our waking thoughts and in our dreams, and then backing away from them. Much of the time we might not reveal these fantasies to anyone else. Sometimes we might not reveal them even to ourselves. We keep them down, refusing to acknowledge their existence. We take a deep breath on the subway platform, join our fellow passengers as we squeeze aboard the train when it finally arrives, and proceed into the evening, going on to suppress all our other aggressive urges, large and small, as they arise—until we don't. The old lady on the platform lives to see another dawn, but the misdelivered alumni magazine that rightfully—and legally—belongs to the neighbor down the hall? Straight down the garbage chute.

Obviously, a crime is not a crime is not a crime. Throwing a stranger into the path of an oncoming train is not the same as throwing a neighbor's mail into the garbage, legally or morally. What's more, a criminal is not a criminal is not a criminal. You or I might never, under any circumstances, push that old woman on the train tracks. But someone else might. All crimes and all criminals nevertheless have something in common: an impulse that has somehow turned into an action that violates the norms of society.

At one extreme of the spectrum are criminals who can't distinguish right from wrong and therefore feel no guilt about their actions. Some criminals in this category suffer from a physical impairment. For instance, a blow to the frontal lobe—a part of the brain that regulates primitive reactions to provocation—can eliminate the gatekeeper that stands between the aggressive impulse and the action. A social worker, a nine-year-old, a lawyer, a schoolteacher—all of them with different personality types and various histories—might suddenly find themselves actually pushing that old woman off the platform, and not caring.

Most criminals who are capable of such actions, however, are suffering not from physical impairment but from a mental illness so severe that they've broken with reality. These people are beyond the reach of reason; they live in a parallel universe defined by their psychosis. Between July 1976 and August 1977, David Berkowitz, the self-proclaimed "Son of Sam," killed six people in New York because a dog told him to. A Texas mother named Andrea Yates drowned her five children because she believed it's what Satan would have wanted.

Sociopaths, by contrast, do distinguish between right and wrong—but they still suffer no guilt for their actions. They can present different selves in different circumstances, and when necessary can act "normal." Such criminals use a highly developed cunning and a chilling emotional detachment in order to prey on their victims. Though the details always change, the "story" is essentially the same: a person, usually male, who finds himself able to see other people as less than human, gets his pleasure by perpetrating acts of astonishing, guilt-free horror. *The end.*

Scott Peterson, a fertilizer salesman in Modesto, California, managed to appear boyish and harmless-looking in front of the cameras after his eight-months-pregnant wife, Laci, went missing on Christmas Eve of 2002, though in fact he had already murdered her and dumped her body into San Francisco Bay. The notorious Ted Bundy could be a real charmer when he wanted to be; throughout the 1970s, he seduced dozens of women in Washington, Utah, Colorado, and Florida, whom he then bludgeoned or strangled. The privileged Menendez brothers, Lyle and Erik, of Beverly Hills, shot their millionaire parents point-blank in order to inherit their money, but looked so young and innocent during their gripping televised trial that viewers sent donations for their defense fund.

"He was a quiet man" is a refrain that friends or neighbors are forever saying about sociopaths after their gruesome crimes have been discovered—as if silence and secrecy are mutually exclusive. "He was a family man" is another favorite remark that's routinely offered with a wondering shake of the head—but, again, what might seem paradoxical in fact makes perfect psychological sense. On a practical level, the role of family man allows a sociopath to blend into the crowd. For thirty years, Dennis Rader lived a relatively quiet life as a husband and father, Cub Scout leader, town ordinance officer, and president of his church before being exposed as the serial killer who signed his taunting letters to the police "BTK"—for "bind, torture, kill," his preferred method for dispatching his victims. But on a deeper level, the role of family man also provides sociopaths with a way to indulge their demons on a daily basis, though in a somewhat socially acceptable way. Behind the raised drawbridge of his castle, Dennis Rader could be king, exercising firm control over his wife and children while also enjoying an outlet for the domineering and sadistic streak that occasionally found full release elsewhere.

Of course, most control freaks aren't murderers, and neither are most quiet people, nor most family men. One of the reasons these extreme cases can command national attention for weeks or months at a time is that they reassure us we could never do what those people do. The most severely mentally ill are proof that "monsters" exist—and we know that we are not monsters. Sociopaths are monsters with a human face—they might look like us, but they're not us. And we're right. We wouldn't push that old woman onto the tracks, and we wouldn't murder a spouse and then coolly join the manhunt for the "killer." But because we all harbor murderous *impulses,* a question lingers long after we've switched off the gavel-to-gavel coverage on Court TV: Are there killers who look like me and could be me?

The evidence isn't flattering. Certainly World War II proved that man's inhumanity to man had not been dented by the passage of time. Studying the defendants in the Nuremberg trials who one after another protested their innocence by saying they were only following orders, the German historian and philosopher Hannah Arendt famously remarked that she had looked upon "the banality of evil." Given the "right" circumstances, people can be led, coaxed, seduced, or bribed to engage in criminal or at least barbaric acts.

In a series of experiments conducted by Stanley Milgram at Yale in the early 1960s, volunteers were recruited from the population of New Haven to engage in a study in which a man sat in a chair that the volunteers had been told was electrically tethered to a dial they controlled. They were also told that the man would be asked a series of questions, and for each one he answered incorrectly, they should give him an electrical shock. They were further instructed that the more wrong answers he gave, the farther they should turn the dial. None of this was true; the subject was an actor. But even as the subject seemed to suffer more intensely from the supposed electric shocks, persuasively convulsing to the brink of losing consciousness, 65 percent of the participants continued to twist the dial as far as it could go—450 volts, easily strong enough to kill anyone.

Few people have their resolve tested under such trying circumstances and at such a visceral level, either during wartime or in a laboratory. Most of us are able to go about our lives under the assumption that we could never do such things, uh-uh, no way, not us. But the murderous impulse is there. It is the id—the part of us that wants what it wants when it wants it—only it is the id at its most naked.

As is always the case with the id, it does constant battle with the ego—the part of us that wants the world to see us the way we ideally see ourselves. And as is always the case in the battle between the id and the ego, the id cannot be eliminated, only accommodated.

At times, the aggressive side of our nature can be sublimated by a so-called positive defense. Someone who joins the armed forces, for instance, may have unconscious wishes to murder; still, he can tell himself he feels only a sense of patriotic duty. The same could be true for a few of the cadets in the police academy. They may have hidden wishes to exert power over everyone, but instead they don badges that allow them to exert power over criminals. Spies can tell themselves that their side is "good" and the other side is "bad," but some spies can't help but feel a kind of kinship with the "enemy." Back in the days of the cold war, *Mad* magazine's "Spy vs. Spy" cartoon embodied this ambiguity on a monthly basis: two pointy-faced figures, one dressed in black and one dressed in white, endlessly trying to destroy each other. Some months, white won; other months, black. Except for the color of their outfits, they were interchangeable.

But accommodating the id doesn't always work. Whenever we hear about the horrors of an unarmed suspect somehow getting shot forty-two times, or a firefighter committing arson, or a spy switching allegiances, or apple-cheeked soldiers committing acts of degradation and sadism and torture, it becomes newly clear that sublimation can be an imperfect defense against an untamed mind.

The fact is, the metaphorical membrane between impulse and action can be thin indeed. Contrary to popular belief, only a very small percentage of violent crimes are committed by people who have suffered a psychotic split or by sociopaths or even by supposedly law-abiding or law-upholding citizens who, when push comes to shove, shove back harder than necessary. In other words, a very small percentage of violent crimes are committed by "not you and not me." Instead, most violent crimes are related to the abuse of alcohol. They're what can happen when we lose our inhibitions—the line of defense that keeps the id in check and the ego intact. Lower that guard and fantasy can quickly become reality, impulse can rage into action.

But even impulses rooted in aggression don't have to end in crimes of violence. There are premeditated crimes—bank robbery, embezzlement, insider trading. There are crimes of opportunity—cheating on taxes, speeding, shoplifting. Sometimes the perpetrators behind these crimes know exactly what they're doing. And sometimes, like Diane the shoplifter, they know *inexactly* what they're doing: They do what they do as if in a daze.

What they do is what counts most in a court of law, not why they do it. If law enforcement officials speak of motive at all, it's usually to figure out the immediate reason: money, rage, revenge. But when psychologists speak of motive, they mean a deeper reason—the unconscious wish that sends serial murderers and serial shoplifters alike right up to the line of lawlessness, and then across it, into the secret life of the criminal.

The threat of punishment is a powerful deterrent to potential criminals. You really might not want to see yourself as someone who would cheat the government or drive drunk or shoplift eyeliner, but you really, *really* might not want to see yourself as someone sitting in a holding cell or being unable to drive for a year or applying for credit with a criminal record.

Punishment, however, can be an equally powerful deterrent after the fact, a constant pressure on the criminal not to breathe a word of the crime to anyone. Criminals are automatic "outsiders" by virtue of their lawbreaking, transgressive activities. As a result, they know that they have to hide their actions if they hope to be allowed the privilege of living among the general population. In a way, the "perp walk"—the ritual whereby the police parade a criminal, whether a lowly drug dealer or a CEO with sticky fingers, from the squad car to the booking station—is a perfect metaphor for this passage. Criminals know that if they get caught they'll move from belonging inside society to belonging outside it. So the criminal mind internalizes an essential message: Don't get caught. *Keep the secret.*

Even the mentally ill who don't differentiate between right and wrong and don't feel guilt, are fearful of a punishment such as prison. Not that they'll see prison as a reflection on the enormity of what they have done or might do; they'll see it instead as a reflection on the enormity of what society wants to do to them. They'll see it as an imposition from the outside world. Still, even they will *see* it—will recognize it as a possibility and adjust their evasions accordingly.

Sociopathic criminals are experts at secrecy. For them, the secret life of the criminal is merely a variation on their dominant theme: the secret life of me. They are not the person they present to the world, and they know it, and they'll do anything to keep that secret identity alive, including murder. Mark Hacking killed his wife, Lori, in Salt Lake City after she learned that he wasn't the aspiring doctor he said he was—that he'd never even graduated from college, let alone been accepted to medical school. Threatened with the destruction of the persona he'd developed—the one his family was so proud of, the one his wife had based her future on—he destroyed Lori instead.

When John List methodically murdered his wife, three children, and mother (who lived with them) in November of 1971, he left behind a letter to his priest saying he feared his family was getting out of his control and would never go to heaven. What he neglected to mention was that he was a fraud and his family was about to find out: He had recently lost his job and could no longer maintain the lifestyle of someone who owned a nineteen-room Victorian mansion in the toniest section of their New Jersey suburb. So powerful was his need to maintain the illusion of who he was that, even after losing his job, he'd continued with his daily routine as if nothing had happened, leaving the house in the morning and heading for the train station, where he would sit and read and pass time until the end of the workday, when he would return home. In the end, John List wound up killing not only his family but himself, in a manner of speaking. He disappeared for nearly two decades, resurfacing only because his case was featured on the television show *America's Most Wanted* and a neighbor recognized him as "Bob Clark," the somewhat nutty neighbor who wore a jacket and tie all the time, taught Sunday school, and had trouble holding on to a job.

Dennis Rader, aka BTK, also managed to hide in plain sight for decades after committing his first murders in the 1970s. But unlike John List, it wasn't someone else who turned him in. It was, in a way, himself. In March 2004, the police received a letter from a supposed "Bill Thomas Killman" that included details and photographs from a 1986 murder, as well as a photocopy of the victim's driver's license; nine months later, BTK wrote the police with details and evidence from another unsolved murder. The tone in the letters was taunting, as if daring the police to catch him—and they did, when they positively traced one of his computer disks to his church.

What ended Dennis Rader's reign of terror might well have been as bewildering to him as what precipitated it. Why send letters and a computer disk if you don't *want* to be caught? And he evidently *did* want to be caught—but not because he felt guilty (sociopaths don't feel guilt), and not because he knew right from wrong (though sociopaths do). He had been a sociopath, and he remained a sociopath. In court, Rader spoke knowledgeably about "serial killers" as a category of which he was a member, much the way that a person with diabetes might give an impromptu lecture to friends about the special medical needs of diabetics. There was no judgment in Rader's voice, no sorrow, and no sense, to listeners, of a person in torment. It was as though Dennis Rader and BTK were relatives, but not the same person.

Instead, the reason Rader "wanted" to be caught is just about the only reason a sociopath would finally surrender a secret identity. He felt he was "bad," though in a way that had nothing to do with the actual commission of his crimes. Confessing to his murders in court, Rader offered that he had "sexual problems"—surely a vast understatement. Still, in that moment he indicated it wasn't the crimes he'd committed that finally drove him into the open. It wasn't *what he'd done*. It was *why he'd done it.*

BTK's predilection for bondage, torture, and murder—and, as it would be revealed, dressing his victims in a "feminine" mask and masturbating over their dead bodies—was no predilection at all, but really an extreme obsession. Though he appears here in a chapter on the secret life of the criminal, he could also fit comfortably in the earlier chapter about perversion. Like all perverts, BTK's need to turn people into inanimate objects was a driving force, and the "roar" of his perversions drowned out the rest of the world. For decades, it was all he could do to control that roar. But by 2004, for reasons we'll probably never know, it was all he *couldn't* do to control it. By then, he felt he needed to be punished not for his crimes but for the reason behind his crimes—his "sexual problems." He was "ready" to be caught.

In this respect, BTK's secret life in particular is representative of the secret life of the criminal in general. It's not that many criminals reach a critical point in their secret lives where they're "ready" to be caught. Most don't in fact trip themselves up; they go to their graves guilty but free. And it's not that criminals (other than the small minority of the severely mentally ill or sociopaths) feel unencumbered by the guilt associated with their crimes. Instead, what unites a case even as extreme as BTK's with that of virtually any other criminal, even our matronly suburban shoplifter Diane, is a lingering feeling of something else—something other than guilt, something equally present yet somehow out of reach, indefinable but defining.

For BTK, as for all criminals, part of this feeling was rage. Whatever the source of his fury might have been, the result was a constant, burning presence, a lifelong companion. Occasionally it would build up until he couldn't bear it, and then he would loose it on some poor innocent victim—a neighbor's dog, perhaps, or a female stranger. And part of the feeling was shame—not for what he'd done because of his sadism, but at what his sadism did to him. It was bigger than him. His perversion crippled him, controlled him, in the way that perversions always do. BTK had acted out his rage by binding, torturing, and killing. And he had acted on his shame by sending out computer disks that exposed him to the full wrath of the law.

Rage? Shame? Surely not *Diane*. She wasn't even a criminal, was she? Just like Jason, the longtime tax cheat from chapter three, who could rationalize every illegal deduction that appeared on his Form 1040, and just like many criminals of opportunity, Diane had her reasons: People do far worse things than shoplift; she's not hurting anyone; these are tiny objects, inexpensive, barely a blip on a store's balance sheet; stores have insurance, anyway. Yet some part of her surely did "know" that what she was doing was a crime. She never stole when a salesperson was standing nearby; she never whispered a word of her habit to her best friend; she never brought out her box of purloined items from her closet to show off to her husband. In this manner, Diane could manage not to be a shoplifter in her mind, yet shoplift indefinitely.

Until, like BTK, she was "ready" to be caught. One day, Diane suddenly made the leap from inexpensive items to a more valuable one, the kind of merchandise that store security is more likely to monitor. Yet even then she didn't remotely recognize that she'd changed her shoplifting habits, let alone why. She'd simply felt the weight of the security guard's hand on her shoulder.

At the local precinct station, a police officer asked Diane why she had taken the dress. She said she didn't know. She was embarrassed to offer such a flimsy defense, and yet the police had heard it before. In fact, if she'd asked them, she would have found out that they'd seen plenty of women like her: women who don't "need" the items they steal; women whose attempts to hide their crimes are at best clumsy, and at worst nonexistent. On retail strips, they're as common as Kinko's, these bizarre, nonneedful shoplifters. To the police, they're a nuisance. To a psychologist interested in the criminal mind, however, they're a source of fascination, a valuable window on how hidden causes can lead to criminal effects.

Though a judge ordered Diane to enter therapy, she came willingly, even eagerly, as though she'd wanted to talk to someone in this way for a long time. I asked her about her life, and she told me that her kids were grown, living settled lives, off on their own.

"So no big changes in recent years?" I wanted to know.

Diane thought about this and shook her head no. Life had been pretty much the same as always. No big changes had taken place. She talked about her kids, expressing the usual mixture of pride and anxieties that most parents feel when their kids are out in the world. The only change, she said after a few moments, concerned her father.

I asked her to tell me more.

She explained that her father had recently been put into a local nursing home, and that she, as the only daughter, was responsible for making sure he was happy and comfortable and well, and for visiting him several times a week. It was "no big deal," Diane maintained.

She said this with a bright smile, but I questioned her further. The job of taking care of an elderly father's every need was taxing, no?

No. No, no, not at all. Diane shook her head vigorously. Then, after a moment, she allowed that maybe at times her father could be a little difficult, like when she'd brought him a new razor a few weeks earlier, and because it wasn't the kind he liked, he casually tossed it into his wastebasket and told her to come back with an "acceptable" one the next day. But her father had always been particular, Diane added.

Even so, she now began to admit to feelings of ambivalence about her father's demands. Before the elderly man had moved to the nursing home, he'd lived independently several hours away, and Diane and her husband had had an idyllic life together. But when her father's increasing age and frailty necessitated the move, Diane had had to quit her part-time job and become his full-time advocate and *de facto* personal assistant. She had said, at the time, that she'd been ready to quit her job anyway, but now she began to wonder if that was true. She missed being the manager of a busy doctor's office. With her father living just a few miles away, Diane was forced to wait on him far more than she'd expected. The small nursing home, when she had initially gone to see it, had seemed like a pretty decent place, with sunny, modern rooms, a friendly staff, and food that was reputed to be far better than the usual nursing-home fare. But since he'd begun living there, her father often complained that the staff did nothing, the food was terrible, and that Diane never brought him the things he asked for. Whether it was a razor or a bathrobe or a selection of new paperbacks she thought he might enjoy, he made it clear that these items were all wrong. His complaints gathered in number and volume, until Diane felt assaulted by them. Her father wasn't just particular, she said; he was critical.

Over time, Diane spoke to me about just how critical her father had been when Diane was a child, lording his own adult status over her, giving her almost no independence whatsoever. He'd acted like a real patriarch, and no one in the family had ever questioned his decisions. Unlike her friends, Diane hadn't been allowed to go out on weekend evenings, even as a teenager. The resentment built up inside her, but she'd never felt that anything her father had done was so "terrible" that she had a right to complain. Instead, she absorbed her feelings of powerlessness and bitterness in the face of an authoritarian and hypercritical father, until over a period of decades they had calcified into something that seemed to have nothing to do with her father whatsoever.

Diane's crimes sprang from a secret that she'd been unable to tell herself throughout her entire life: that she was furious with her impossible father and wished she could get back at him for keeping such tight control over her throughout childhood, adolescence, and now, once again, middle age. But Diane was a "good" daughter, and found it difficult to imagine herself telling her father off. After all, her father was an elderly man in a nursing home, and what kind of person yelled and screamed at an eighty-two-year-old man with a walker? What kind of ungrateful person could even *think* such a thing? Not *Diane*.

But she was, in fact, a person who could think such a thing, just as she was, in fact, a criminal. Just like BTK, she felt rage. For years the fury of being controlled by her father had been building up. Her marriage had offered her a decades-long reprieve, but now her father was back in her life with a vengeance. And just like BTK, Diane felt shame—shame at feeling such rage at someone she was supposed to love. She had acted out her rage by shoplifting, in effect defying all the controlling fathers out there in the world. And she had acted on her shame by ensuring that she would be caught and brought to justice—not just in a court of law, but in the court of her unconscious.

Humans seek to rectify wrongs in various ingenious ways. Sometimes, a dress must be stolen from a rack in order for a grown daughter to regain a sense of personal power and dignity. And sometimes, the ways these long-suppressed emotions reach the surface are far worse than that. Innocent women must be murdered because of a man's shameful feelings about sex, and his mother, and women, and his own hateful self. Money must be stolen from banks, cash registers, strangers' purses. Houses must be set on fire. The world sometimes seems to explode with its own wildfire of unchecked violence. Secrets, while providing temporary shelter for a criminal, time and again serve to fan the flames of ambivalence, conflict, and aggression.

Diane, though, was fortunate in two ways. Unlike many criminals, she hadn't committed crimes of a caliber or in a quantity that ruined her life. And unlike most criminals, she was able to get the kind of therapy that allowed her to figure out why she'd done what she did—and freed her from the compulsion to do it again.

Diane made the decision to speak to her father about his behavior and set up some ground rules for her visits. She would come see him once or twice a week, at most, she told him; after all, he'd made good friends at the nursing home, and whenever she came, he was always sitting among a group of other men. She would take requests for items he needed every week, but he was to treat her choices respectfully, or she would stop bringing him things. He seemed startled. He'd never heard her speak to him in such a forthright and impassioned manner. And even though he insisted he didn't know what she was talking about, he really did, of course, and in the end he didn't put up much resistance.

One day on the drive home after visiting her father, Diane stopped at the mall for the first time since her arrest. She walked in and out of stores and, to her relief, felt no desire to take anything. She bought a small item that she needed and then headed for home. The trip was uneventful, manageable, civilized. On this expedition, at least, the mall wasn't a jungle at all.

[9 • THE SECRET LIFE, EXAMINED]

Hell is other people.

—Jean-Paul Sartre, *No Exit* (1944)

Whatever happened to Scott, the software evangelist from chapter three, who became addicted to watching pay-per-view porn while staying in hotel rooms? For some men, an ongoing taste for pornography can be maintained over a long period of time. But for Scott, the rewards diminished as the months passed. Eventually all the movie watching and ritual masturbation became predictable and tame, and was no longer enough to give him the happy, postorgasmic satiety he'd come to expect. He found himself slightly indifferent to the women who writhed and arched on the TV screen, and he wished there was something he could do to counteract this response. One night, he took his rental car and drove around an unfamiliar city, stopping in at a concrete strip club for a lap dance. But he didn't like being out there in such a stale, unsavory place, and preferred the safety and comfort of his hotel room.

So the next time Scott traveled, he ended up flipping through the yellow pages that he found in the drawer of the night table, right beside the Bible. He located *E* for "Escort Services," and soon he was on the telephone with a woman from a place called Premiere Ladies, giving out his room number at the hotel. Forty minutes later, someone called Amber Lynn was at his door. She was pretty much what he'd expected: blonde with roots showing, one of those orangey tanning-salon tans, and a pair of plumped-up breasts that had certainly been created on a surgical table. But he didn't care. Just the idea of her being here in his hotel room aroused him. She could have been anyone, and it wouldn't have mattered.

Scott lay on the floral bedspread with Amber Lynn and let her straddle him and then let her perform oral sex. He didn't have to worry about paying her, because he'd already given out his credit-card number over the telephone, being sure to bill the expense to a separate account he had opened for "emergencies." The experience turned out to be everything he wanted—all the illicit excitement, the high, the thrilling secretiveness, that pay-per-view porn had once provided.

It was an experience he repeated again and again in the months that followed. Hiring escorts for sex became as much a part of Scott's travel routine as filling out the room-service breakfast menu and leaving it on the doorknob. He folded these women into his trips. They enhanced the experience of travel, work, and life in general. The initial boredom that had caused him to take action had been paved over with a renewed vigor. He seemed to work harder in meetings the morning after he'd been with an escort, and to push himself further on the treadmill at the hotel gym. Having a secret life even helped at home, he told himself. He found he was able to be more loving and expansive with his wife, Lisa. Sometimes after sex, when the escort had already left, he would lie on his back in bed in the half dark and telephone his wife. They would speak gently and lovingly to each other in sleepy voices, saying "I love you" at the end and sending each other kisses.

Then, after hanging up, Scott would check his Palm Pilot to see where he'd be traveling next, and he would find himself wondering what the escort services were like in Albuquerque or Denver or Pittsburgh.

To reveal or conceal: that is the question. Most people experience the tension between these impulses on a daily basis, in both mundane and serious ways. Do you tell the cashier that she gave you too much change? Do you let your elderly mother know she has inoperable cancer? For someone whose secrets have gathered enough force and transformed into a fully realized secret life, the emphasis is always on concealment, which in and of itself becomes an active task. People who live secret lives spend blocks of time and a great deal of energy thinking about and worrying over and imagining what it would be like to be found out. Their hearts race with anxiety as they envision the scenario, and with good reason. For when a secret life is suddenly discovered, all hell breaks loose.

Hell, of course, can mean different things to different people. Sometimes the shame of exposure is enough to destroy a person, even if the actual repercussions of discovery are few. Other times, merely having to withstand intense scrutiny can seem unbearable. When Bill Clinton's secret Oval Office life with Monica Lewinsky was exposed to the entire world, he almost lost the presidency. The intense fascination with—and, in some quarters, pleasure at—his disgrace, wasn't just because he'd acted in a sexually inappropriate way with someone whose name wasn't Hillary. It was also because he'd dared to be so powerful in the first place. *Tough luck, buddy,* came the message, *you thought you could have it all: power, a big house,* Air Force One, *the ability to press the button on the suitcase, as well as a woman who will come into your office and open your fly whenever you want. But guess what? You can't have it all.* Martha Stewart's crime was met with a similar kind of response: a mixture of empathy and shock along with a feeling of triumph. *You think you can bake raspberry pies better than me, and make papier-mâché candlesticks, and have a zillion-dollar empire, and find a sneaky way to get richer than you already are. Well, guess what, lady? You've got another think coming.*

Though it's certainly a part of human nature—if not a pretty part—to want to watch people suffer, other emotional elements are at work in these instances. It's a relief to feel that someone *else* is going down, not us, because we can all imagine a scenario in which we, too, might behave in a shocking manner, and we can imagine this so clearly because we all have our secrets, even if they never become known around the world.

The revelation of some secrets is tolerable though embarrassing, and everyone has had such small, eruptive episodes: being singled out at work by your employer for not handing in a project; having your mother find a love letter you wrote. They're awful in the moment, and you twist in the wind and feel as though you're going to die on the spot. And then, miraculously, you *don't* die. Your employer, having excoriated you briefly, moves on to something else. Your mother understands that you're an adolescent whose insides are a soup of intense emotions, and she doesn't mention the love letter ever again.

But there are other secrets that we'll do anything to keep from being exposed because of what we fear they say about us. What that *is*, however, might well be a secret even from ourselves. It is concealing this secret from ourselves that leads directly to the creation of a secret life. The hell that breaks loose here is not just what the *world* would think, but the fact that once the secret is out, we know we're going to be forced to examine ourselves in a way we've been avoiding for as long as we can remember.

No one can know the secrets from the self that Bill Clinton carried around, even if *we* carry around his 1,008-page autobiography. It's likely that he still doesn't know them, either. The same was true of Scott, at least at first. By his own admission, he'd never spent much time analyzing his actions. Instead, he'd created, for his own purposes, a supposed reason for hiring escorts—"boredom"—and satisfied with this explanation, he then pursued his agenda without much self-doubt or insight.

Scott knew he was a secret-keeper, but he never knew he had another layer of secrets—or at least, he wasn't fully aware that he did. Then came the day he returned home from a trip to Albuquerque and found his wife sitting at the kitchen table in tears. What was she doing home? Why wasn't she at work? Why was she in tears? Was someone sick? Had someone died?

And then Scott knew. One look at what his wife had spread out before her on the table told him all he needed to know: his private Visa-card statements.

What could he say? He had absolutely no defense. Denial is the handiest and most useful mechanism for secret-keepers in danger of being exposed. Both Bill Clinton and Martha Stewart denied everything they'd been accused of. If the words are uttered forcefully enough ("I did not have sexual relations with that woman"), then other people may just begin to believe them. Especially in the case of a public figure like Bill Clinton, maintaining a belief in heroes allows us to keep certain fantasies alive. Clinton, as president, served as a father figure to an entire nation, and, in a sense, to the world. What kind of father would get his kicks in such a tawdry way, even die-hard Democrats asked themselves, and then dissemble about it? Not *my* father. But Scott didn't have the option of denial. Evidence was laid out before him on the table.

Lisa was furious, her eyes blazing. In those first moments, husband and wife faced each other in the kitchen in silence. Lisa didn't say anything; she didn't have to. Then Scott simply said, "Oh, shit," and felt his heart race and his face flush with blood. For the next few hours, Lisa called him every name she could think of; he'd never once heard her speak like that in all the years they'd been together. The facts were all there in black and white: itemized statements listing every last one of his purchases from Ladies on Demand of Rockville, Maryland, or Capital Escorts of Detroit. And Scott couldn't deny that every name Lisa called him was absolutely dead-on accurate. Scott was someone who had deliberately, methodically, and repeatedly cheated on his wife over a period of many months, paying women to perform lewd acts on him, and performing lewd acts on them as well.

It wasn't just the sex, though, that horrified Lisa. It was the emotional connection that he'd made to these women through being naked in front of them, and seeing them naked, too. A kind of intimacy exists even in the most anonymous sex, and Lisa could not forgive him for engaging in such intimacy. Ten years earlier, Scott and Lisa had stood on a hill of wildflowers in front of two hundred witnesses and one priest and promised never to betray each other. It had been easy to say those words, and for an entire decade it had been easy to live by them. Now Scott had broken that promise in an outrageous way, and he deserved any name Lisa might care to call him. If she made him sleep on the couch for a few weeks, so be it. He would apologize forever. He would make it up to her in every way he could.

And it wasn't just the betrayal of intimacy. It was the betrayal of *trust* that enraged her—and frightened her, too. "Who are you?" she viciously whispered at Scott. "Who are you?" How could she ever be sure what was true in her life and what wasn't? And how could she not have seen? It was right there, all the evidence, all along, but somehow she had turned a blind eye. How could she ever trust him again? How could she ever trust anyone? How could she ever trust *herself*—her own sense of what was real, and what was not?

The accusations were flying faster and faster; Scott could barely keep up with the intensity and volume of her rage. She was blaming him. She was blaming herself. Scott wanted to interrupt her at any number of moments, but he didn't dare; he wanted to tell her that she was being too hard on herself. He wanted to tell her, *Blame me. Hit me if you want. Hit me even if you don't want—I deserve it anyway. I deserve whatever punishment you or anyone else wants to mete out. I have been a schmuck, a loser, low-life scum.*

But do I really have to stop seeing those women?

As his wife screamed and cried in this furious, anguished voice, his thoughts couldn't help but drift back to the woman he'd been with the night before. Her name was Ginger, she'd told him, and her hair was a light brown gingery color. She had been vulnerable and beautiful as she bent her head down over his lap. He would never see her again, or anyone like her. And when he thought of this, he shared his wife's level of anguish.

Some tiny part of Scott even resented the fuss Lisa was making over this. After all, everything had worked so well when she was kept in the dark. Their marriage had been solid, and he was an involved husband and father. There were financial considerations to hiring escorts so frequently, but Scott had thought that all through, and made sure that his salary could absorb the cost. And of course he wore condoms during sex; he wasn't about to contract a disease. She didn't have to worry about that.

Why couldn't Lisa have found the credit-card statement and then put it back where he'd left it? Other wives would have done just that. She shouldn't have been snooping in his files to begin with. Why couldn't she just accept the fact that, like some men, Scott needed women in his life and in his bed? Lots of women, all kinds of them, for he was a heterosexual male in his prime. The only things these escorts had in common were that all of them were paid and all of them were virtually anonymous. He had no real relationship with them outside the sex; he didn't ask them to tell him touching stories from their childhood. Nor were they interested in him. They had "names," but most were clearly self-invented. These women had probably not been born Amber Lynn or Ginger. He had no idea who they really were, and they had no idea who he was, and that was what made it work so well.

But Lisa had changed that. In one swift moment, Scott's freedom and anonymity and pleasure had been ripped away for good.

Anyone whose secret has been forced out into the open—or anyone who voluntarily makes a confession—has to ask the question "Now what?" At this point, flight is still an option. The secret life, after all, is in the fight of its life, struggling for its very survival. Under such inner pressure, the secret-keeper might find ingenious ways to go on maintaining that the secret *isn't* in fact a secret, or isn't an important secret, or isn't his or her fault, anyway. Or else the secret-keeper can try to find a creative way to seal up the potential leak and limit the external damage.

Some people turn to new and improved modes of denial and acting out. A college student who faces expulsion after his plagiarism has been discovered by school officials might call his parents and say, "Well, you always insisted I had to be perfect. You *led* me to plagiarize, and it's all your fault." This rationalization allows the secret-keeper to keep a safe distance from whatever actually motivated the behavior. It was a close call, but now the student won't have to wrangle with his own unconscious wishes and destructive impulses after all.

It also helps to have someone else on hand who will back the story up, particularly someone who keeps the environment hospitable to secrets—someone we call a "secret-enabler." This sidekick may be unaware of his or her own knowledge, yet automatically act on it anyway. A woman whose husband has been secretly spending all his time and salary at the local OTB may be sure to leave him alone on the weekend, saying she's busy with her own errands. An elderly man whose wife has recently been diagnosed with type 2 diabetes may somehow always be out of the room at the times when his wife heads into the pantry to secretly eat foods she's no longer allowed.

This was the case with Scott. His wife never pressed him for details about his traveling life; in this way, she could continue to enable his pattern of infidelity, and to find a way to "know" that something odd was going on with her husband, and yet also "not know," too. They made quite a pair, working in lockstep. If he seemed loving but somehow vague lately, and if their own sex life had withered over time, she chalked it up to how busy they both were, and to how they'd reached a certain age at which sex in a marriage has become less important.

The secret-enabler also may *consciously* know about the lie. In that case, his or her role is to help maintain the secret. This creates a feeling of power and membership in some exclusive club. A special intimacy is forged, along the lines of: *You and I are the only ones on the face of the earth who know the real story*. But there's another, subtler message there, too: *Other than you, I am the only person who knows the real story, so you'd better treat me right*. The secret-enabler has a threat in his or her pocket, which may or may not actually be taken out and used. But it's there, and both parties know it.

Many people looked suspiciously at Hillary Clinton during the

Monica Lewinsky affair, convinced that her wifely outrage over her husband's conduct was manufactured, and that she'd known exactly what was going on, and always had, from Gennifer Flowers on. A "pact" had been made between Bill and Hillary, some surmised, the way it's often made between secret-keepers and their enablers. Secrets link people inextricably; the only way the connection might be severed is if the secret itself comes to light. In some instances, that can take a lifetime or two. Or maybe even three. Family secrets—incest, alcoholism, mental illness, to name just a few—are routinely passed down from one generation to another like something in a gothic novel, with no one in the family willing to expose the dreaded secret to outside eyes, and everyone tacitly enabling one another in this elaborate, clannish cover-up.

Sometimes, when a secret life does get exposed, it was actually *ready* to die, and exposure isn't all that hellish. When the pain of keeping it alive becomes greater than the pain of surrendering its existence, then the revelation of the secret can create a sensation of release. *Now I don't have to worry so much,* the exposed secret-keeper might feel. *All the lying, all the covering up—I'm done with that.* The exposure of a long-held secret can provide a quick, intense catharsis, a dip in an icy pool after living in a stuffy, overheated room for far too long. The cycle of needing to conceal but wanting to reveal, of wanting to reveal but needing to conceal, has finally been broken.

The bracing plunge into truth, though, is merely the first step. *Now what?* continues past this phase, and into whatever lies ahead.

Depending on how brave the former secret-keeper feels, *now what?* might include the revelation, at long last, of the secrets that have been kept from the self.

Scott, for example, had carefully maintained a dividing line between his relationship with female escorts and all other relationships in his life. Now that line had been stepped across, creating a direct threat to his marriage. But more frighteningly—and less visibly to him at first—there was also the possibility of a violation to the *inner* boundary. This was the one that Scott had hammered up between himself and his unconscious, allowing him to not really "know" why he was having these relationships with women, or to grasp the full effect of his actions.

Plenty of people do this every day, in both dramatic and subtle ways. They don't want to face the reasons behind their own actions, and so they create for themselves a level of awareness that hovers between the conscious and the unconscious: a convenient state of subconscious realization in which they have to face only what they can handle, and nothing more. In this middle state, a man may tell himself his chronic infidelity is harmless. A woman might find a lump in her breast while taking a shower, but allow herself to assume it's nothing by the time the shower's over, and then "forget" about it entirely.

Even if the choice to reveal a secret to the world was involuntary, what happens next is up to the former secret-keeper, who can choose to tell a glib, shallow version of the story, or a deeper, *truer* version that is sure to have repercussions both inside and out. The main way that someone can begin to grapple with the truth is through talking about it honestly. And the most useful and safest place to do such talking is in a therapist's office.

Throughout this book, we've looked at various instances of people entering therapy, but until now we've never really examined the specific kind of back-and-forth that takes place there. Scott's therapy was no more typical than anyone else's, but his experience illustrates how a willing participant can come to terms not only with the secret life he kept from the outside world, but with the secret life he unknowingly lived within himself.

Scott first came to see me two weeks after Lisa had confronted him about the escorts. He'd slept on the couch in the den every night since she'd found the credit-card receipts. His daily interaction with his wife was perfunctory, and then one morning Lisa announced in a formal voice that the only way she would consider staying married was if he went into therapy. Scott tried to argue, telling her he'd never been in therapy before and didn't really think he was the kind of person who would get much out of it.

"Fine," Lisa said. "Then you can move out tomorrow. Good luck with your new life."

So entering therapy hadn't been a choice. But what he did in therapy—what he spoke about, confronted, and ultimately learned about himself—was up to him. When Scott entered my office he was both angry and nervous. When I asked him to tell me what had brought him here, he replied, "Lisa. My wife. It's because of her that I'm here. Otherwise, believe me, I'd be far, far away." We discussed her ultimatum, and he said he felt like a little kid who'd been called into the principal's office. When I asked him to say more about this feeling, Scott seemed surprised. "I can't see that it's all that relevant," he said, and he went on to tell me he'd assumed that we would talk only about his habit of hiring escorts, and that I'd "rap him on the knuckles," the way Sister Anne, the principal of his Catholic elementary school, used to do when he was a boy.

I told him that psychoanalysts believe that all thoughts that occur to a patient during a session are in some way relevant and potentially useful, and so, with a heavy sigh, he began to talk a little bit about Catholic school, and about his current household, which he said was "run" by a woman far different from Sister Anne.

"Different how?" I asked.

"I don't know, just different," he replied, and his voice betrayed a certain level of irritation, as though he'd suddenly remembered that he was here in a therapist's office only because his wife wanted him to be here, and not because he thought anything was really wrong with him. Scott was resistant to therapy, because he'd thought it was for people who liked to "navel-gaze." He admitted that he resented having to pay hard-earned money just to have "an interesting conversation."

But therapy isn't just made up of interesting conversation. Sometimes it does include an engaging and rapid back-and-forth, but those sessions are often no more valuable than the ones that are halting and awkward in spots. Silences in the middle of a therapy session reveal that something is going on underneath that can't yet be spoken. Scott and I came upon a few of those silences early on, but time after time he insisted that *nothing* was happening, and that there wasn't anything he couldn't talk about.

As the weeks passed, we often found ourselves at a kind of standstill.

"I get the feeling," I told him one day, "that you're here in body but not in spirit. Even now, I don't think you've gotten past that view of me as an authority figure who wants to punish you."

"You and Lisa both," he said quietly. "How long is she going to keep it up? This martyr thing is getting a little old."

I asked him if he thought Lisa was taking her anger too far, and he nodded. "Haven't I told her I'm sorry?" he said, his voice getting louder and his face reddening. "Haven't I sent her flowers, and taken the kids to the park on Sundays, and come here every week like a good little boy? What more does she want from me?"

I let his question hang there, and once again there was silence, but this time we both settled into it. *What more does she want from me?* This was a question that hinted at another, more important question, which was: *What more do I want from myself?* And, relatedly:

Why am I really here in Dr. Saltz's office? Why did I need those women so badly that I was willing to risk everything?

"Do you still want to see those women?" I asked.

To his own surprise, Scott found himself in tears. He put his face in his hands briefly, then looked up at me. "I have no idea why I'm crying," he said. Then, he added ruefully, "Frankly, Dr. Saltz, I don't know why I do *anything* that I've done for the past year."

I wish I could say that Scott achieved one rapid-fire epiphany after another that allowed him to see what had led him on this strange, zigzag path from having sex in hotel beds with other women, to sleeping on the couch in his den, to sitting on a chair in a psychiatrist's office. But only in movies does therapy work in such a direct and reliable way. Scott was still angry at Lisa for her ultimatum, even as he had been chastened by her discovery and immediately willing to try to help his marriage. His anger, over the months that he was my patient, attached itself to many subjects. When he talked about women, he was sometimes mocking and cutting. He referred to a coworker as "a bitch," and when I questioned him about it, he became defensive.

"Come on, I love women," he said. "Obviously." He gave a little laugh. "I mean, I wound up here because I love them too much."

Silence again. The words sounded hollow, and he knew they did, so Scott followed up a few seconds later. "I guess paying women for sex doesn't sound to you like love," he said.

"Does it sound like it to you?"

"Ah, the old therapist trick people always talk about," he said. "Turning the question around on the patient. But okay, I'll bite. What I felt with those escorts—well, no, it wasn't love. But I treated them well. Sometimes I would walk them down to the lobby and we'd get a drink in the bar afterward, and we'd just talk before they went home. . . ." His voice trailed off.

"You sound sad right now," I remarked.

"Yeah, I guess I miss them," Scott said, his voice tightening. He started to say something else, then stopped himself.

"What were you going to say?" I asked.

"Nothing." Another silence. And then: "I don't know, I just remembered that when I was little, my mom would come into my bedroom sometimes at night and bring me a glass of water."

With encouragement, Scott described the closeness of sitting with his beautiful mother in his dark bedroom. He recalled feeling slightly aroused once as she sat there, and then becoming ashamed of himself. "I mean, I was kind of turned on, and she was reading me *Charlotte's Web* or something. It's kind of sick. I wasn't even going to bring it up."

But I told him I was glad he had. And he brought it up again and again over time in therapy, and the anecdote took on other details, feeding into other anecdotes, other details and memories. Scott's mother was a very sexual woman, often dressing provocatively at home—supposedly for her husband's pleasure, but her three sons happened to live in the house, too. Scott remembered his father being proud at times of his wife's sexual allure, but on other occasions growing suddenly furious with her.

"Change your dress!" his father had shouted one night when the couple was about to head out to a dinner party and he'd seen the black strapless number she had on. "I wanted to punch him out for being so cruel to her," Scott said. "Maybe the dress was kind of inappropriate, I don't know. But I liked that she had this sexy aura about her, and you know what? My dad liked it, too. How was she supposed to know when he was going to go, 'Hey, I like that,' and when he was going to say, 'You slut.' "

The word hung in the air: *slut*.

"He never used the word," Scott said. "I don't mean that."

But he did, of course. And as we continued to talk, Scott spoke about how as a child he'd often felt confused about the images of his mother that seemed to change so freely depending on what she was wearing and how his father responded to her. Sometimes she was a "goddess" in Scott's father's eyes; at other times he belittled her, saying she "dressed like a hooker," and then she would run off crying to the bedroom for the night. Scott could hear her sobs, and he would pound on the door, begging her to let him in, but she never did. "Go away, Scott," she'd tell him. "There's nothing you can do to help."

"But there is!" he cried once when this happened. "I'll get you some Chips Ahoy!" He ran to the kitchen and put some cookies on a plate, hoping that somehow they would make his mother feel better. But they didn't, of course. The cookies remained untouched, and his mother would retreat into herself, sitting alone with no makeup on in a dowdy bathrobe, mending one of the kids' socks or making a shopping list. Scott would try to talk to her, tell her jokes, get her to engage with him, but she was always quiet and uninterested in his attentions. "Have you done your homework?" was all she would say mildly. Or: "Go upstairs and pack for that field trip tomorrow." She was like a prim and docile 1950s housewife in these moments, and not at all the free-spirited 1970s woman he'd seen so recently. All traces of that sexual side were gone, only to roar back a few days later, when she dressed up sexily for an evening out. And the whole cycle would begin all over again.

"I didn't know how to see her," he said quietly in my office one afternoon. "My vision of her would change drastically. She'd be either all sexy and kind of free, or else sort of conservative and restrained." As we talked about these early experiences with his mother, he came to feel that even now, decades after he was a small boy banging on a bedroom door, he still needed to find a way to split his images of women into two halves: "good" and "bad." This hadn't been possible with his image of his wife, whom he had always cast as unfailingly conservative and "good"; this, in fact, was partly why he had been drawn to her in the first place. A "good" wife allowed him to manage his long-standing ambivalence toward women. Lisa satisfied the need for a "good" woman, a "mom" figure, while his other needs for a "sexualized," "bad" woman went unsatisfied for a long time.

In therapy, Scott looked directly at his ambivalence toward

women, and recognized how he'd compartmentalized his feelings toward them. Compartmentalizing had seemed, for a while, to allow him to get everything he needed: a loving mother figure at certain moments, and a sexually adventurous partner at others. The split was a perfect echo of his confusing, split view of his mother when he was a little boy. As Scott explored these issues, he wondered whether he could approach Lisa directly and see whether she'd be willing to experiment a bit more in bed. He'd never given her a clue that this was what excited him; he'd never dared ask her if she'd be willing to try new things. And he came to realize now that he had never asked her because he'd been afraid that if he did, her role as the "good" figure would diminish, and he'd be left without someone comforting and maternal. They soon entered couples therapy; the point wasn't so much to see if Lisa could comply with Scott's desires, but to see if they both could find ways to satisfy each other.

Scott's actions had threatened his marriage, but so, too, had his fiercely guarded blindness to his own desires. This blindness had allowed him to keep his secrets intact, and those secrets in turn had become more potent. What was malignant had metastasized. But when secrets from the self are exposed to the light and looked at without condemnation, they lose much of their force. The great and powerful Oz simply becomes the man behind the curtain. But he *should* be paid attention to. Scott had maintained that he'd come to his secret life almost by accident; he was "bored," so he'd watched a porno movie. And then the porno just hadn't cut it for him, and he required something stronger. One thing led to another, and soon Scott was giving out his credit-card number over the phone night after night and opening his hotel-room door to greet the next woman who awaited him.

Scott's early impressions of his mother and father and the ways he processed these ideas over time had created a template for how his adult self viewed women. As a result, he compulsively acted out his strong but static fantasies again and again. Therapy let him look at his fantasies without flinching so often, and eventually it loosened them from their moorings. What made his therapy work—what makes *any* therapy work—was a motivation to change. Perhaps you know the joke "How many psychiatrists does it take to change a lightbulb? None. The lightbulb has to *want* to change."

Once in therapy, a secret-keeper needs to keep two metaphorical "windows" open concurrently. The first is the emotional window, the one through which the patient describes and experiences the strong feelings associated with the secret behavior. Looking at his life through this window, Scott told me all about the pleasure of sex with prostitutes. He described it in detail, recounting the moments of conquest and the deep and easy peace he felt upon climax. The secret-keeper needs to be able to describe the moment-by-moment sensations of his or her actions, and also tell the therapist what memories are triggered, and what emotions are summoned from the past. Ideally, looking through this window will allow the secret-keeper to identify certain feelings from long ago that were repressed and eventually led to "copycat" feelings and behaviors that had to be kept secret in order to be maintained. This is a window into the past, unsanitized and unedited, and definitely unflattering.

Fortunately, there's also a second window. This is the intellectual window, the one that allows the patient to act almost as a field anthropologist, observing behavior. What's that guy doing with that woman? How often does he do it? *Why* does he do it? What if he no longer got to do it? And as he asks these questions, he remains amazingly unthreatened by all the dark, unpredictable, often sexual behavior he's witnessing. He just sits there observing, taking notes and occasionally saying something to the effect of "Wow, it's really interesting what happened to me back then, and it's equally interesting that I behave in such a way now. I'm starting to see how my early experiences led me to go to such extremes and risk so much that matters to me."

Scott did exactly this as he recounted his early feelings of erotic excitement in his mother's presence, and the anger he felt on his mother's behalf when his father belittled her. Soon he was able to link these moments from childhood with recent events from adulthood. Keeping both these windows open requires a great deal of determination and desperation on the part of the patient, and a great deal of guidance from the therapist. Good therapy helps a person shuttle back and forth between the two views of the self, moving from one to the other in order to experience and observe, experience and observe, and finally to start to make inferences from all that reliving and all that observation.

When Scott first entered therapy, he claimed to want to save his marriage, but this was only rhetoric. Saving his marriage required looking at his own behavior, and he was unable to do that in any meaningful way until the day he found himself in tears in my office. That session gave him the first glimmer of light. It was only then that he was able to go beyond his own empty words. The windows opened.

Though therapy is one of the only avenues for resolution after a highly secret life has been exposed, not everyone can make use of it. Success or failure depends on the severity of the person's secrets, as well as the amount of pain involved and the pressure that's been placed on him or her to deal with the situation. It also depends upon a person's inner resources. A psychiatrist has to assess the fundamental intactness of a person's basic sense of self. If it seems in one piece rather than fragmented and disorganized, then the person can be expected to tolerate the deep and sometimes traumatic work of therapy.

T. E. Lawrence would probably not have been able to endure such therapy or been helped by it. His need to be whipped and beaten as a means to fulfillment, or even his insistence that he had been whipped by a sadistic officer at Deraa, points to a very deep and intractable pathology. From a visual standpoint, life ideally should be like a movie, filled with many kinds of images to excite the mind and the senses. Though in fact Lawrence's external life was so elaborate that it was turned into a big-budget Hollywood movie, his interior life may well have resembled a slide show, with only one slide stuck in the carousel: the picture of that whip. The static nature of T. E. Lawrence's sadomasochism and the fact that it substituted for mutual, human, sexual relationships suggest that he would have been resistant to any kind of therapy, no matter how much he suffered, and would have been in danger of crumbling emotionally upon being confronted. Battle, desert heat, brutality, bloodshed: All of that was tolerable to the world-famous Lawrence of Arabia. But confronting certain truths about himself—the fathomless depths of his rage at his abusive mother, perhaps—was out of the question.

Pyotr Tchaikovsky would not have been helped by therapy, either, though for a different reason. The composer's problems weren't caused by any pathology of his own; he was a productive, brilliant man who found pleasure and passion in music and who knew he was sexually attracted to men and acted on his desires. While he experienced shame and self-loathing at his sexuality and advised his homosexual younger brother to marry, these reactions were a reflection of the freely expressed hostility toward homosexuals that was overflowing in nineteenth-century Russian society. Why *wouldn't* a homosexual feel that he deserved to die or to be banished to Siberia? After all, everyone said that he did. The tragedy of Tchaikovsky's story and many others like it lies in the powerlessness of the individual to change or overcome external forces.

But when the forces that guide a person are internal and seemingly within reach, then movement is possible. As with Diane, the middle-aged woman who was arrested for shoplifting, Scott was emotionally intact and articulate and made a reasonable candidate for therapy. When he thought about what he had done, he agreed that something other than boredom had to be underneath his involvement with prostitutes. And then he also understood that for the sake of his wife, his children, and himself, he had to try to discover what it was.

Most people's secret lives aren't as extreme as some of these stories. Husbands stray, but not usually so systematically and expensively as Scott did. Serial killers are rare, homosexuality has become more accepted in many parts of the United States, Canada, and Europe, and support groups exist nowadays for almost every imaginable addiction. The majority of secret lives aren't as scandalous as they would have been at an earlier point in time, though society still has a distinct taste for punishing secret-keepers, Hester Prynne style.

Over and over, the secrets that get people into the greatest trouble tend to be the ones that remain pushed down into the depths of the unconscious, where they fester and cause their keepers to act out instead of understand. Destruction can often follow, with the secret-keeper standing in the epicenter of the "earthquake" and looking around in bewilderment, wondering, "How did this happen to me?"

But not always. Though the dangers of unresolved conflicts and their relation to secrets have been detailed in the stories told in these chapters, many secret lives are normal, even healthy. And most secrets, even when revealed, don't require therapy. A woman might enjoy spanking her partner once in a while during sex; that's a secret that she may not want revealed, but it provides her with a kind of private pleasure that invigorates her sexual life from time to time and never overwhelms or transforms it. An undeclared crush on someone can also be a healthy and useful secret, especially given the fact that fantasy isn't the same as action. A crush, too, is different from an obsession, and can often be incorporated into a repertoire of various erotic thoughts that float through the mind on a daily or nightly basis. Sometimes, a secret of the nondestructive variety might simply be a piece of information that someone chooses not to share for personal reasons. A woman might not tell her husband that long ago, before she met him, she had an abortion. Such reticence, while associated with conflicted feelings, is her choice. The secret can remain a secret, in no way unhealthy, as long as she isn't plagued by doubts about her actions so long ago.

Remember the woman nattering away in the doctor's waiting room? Maybe *her* secret isn't that she's dying, but just that she's nervous around doctors.

And that man on the treadmill at the gym? Maybe his secret is simply that he's going to propose to his girlfriend tonight.

And the husband who turns to you in bed? Maybe his only secret is that he's missed you all day, and couldn't wait for you to return.

People's lives are studded with close-to-the-vest wishes, needs, and fantasies. What the healthy ones can *do,* in the best of circumstances, is allow people to keep slivers of themselves away from the reach of the rest of the world. Secrets can create a small but necessary clearing in the midst of a dense forest, a space for being creative and (paradoxically) honest, at least with the self. Secrets make people aware of what's most precious to them, and let them take stock of their lives in ways they might not otherwise be able to. Scott was able to face the various conflicts of his past, and so was Diane the shoplifter, and as a result not only did they survive the respective crises that were the direct result of the force of their secrets, but their lives were made more meaningful for it.

So, in the end, is the secret life really worth the anxiety and the emotional cost of its upkeep? Some former secret-keepers would undoubtedly do it all over again in exactly the same way, if given the chance, but those who have been able to use the trauma of exposure as a way to achieve authenticity might just say that secrets are merely temporary shelter against the storm that is self-awareness. And they might go on to conclude that an examined—and candid—life is the only kind worth living.

[Afterword • THE SECRET LIFE, EXPOSED]

If an examined and candid life is the only one worth living, how do we learn to live it? The question becomes even more complicated if the life we are trying to examine candidly is a *secret* life. How are we to find these secrets, let alone examine them? The wall is wide, the wall is high, the wall is thick. Yet here I am, encouraging you to see what's on the other side. I don't know what's there, of course. Secret lives are as varied as the people who live them. But I do think it's possible to find out what's there.

I can't promise that this process will be pain-free. As we've seen repeatedly throughout this book, a secret life doesn't come from nowhere. It can arise out of the deepest conflicts in a person's past. Addressing that secret life inevitably involves uncovering those conflicts, requires crossing over into the unconscious and seeking out the source of the pain and confusion that have compelled the secret-keeper to lead two lives. Yet only by working through that pain can you be free of it. Only by coming to terms with what is causing the pain will you be able to overcome it.

IF SOMEONE YOU KNOW IS LIVING A SECRET LIFE

There are signs and clues that suggest someone you know might be living a secret life, but clues are not conclusive evidence. Your husband, for instance, might be moody or distracted, but that doesn't necessarily mean he's cheating on you. Finding him in bed with a neighbor, however, does. Still, these warning signs are a start.

Let's begin with emotional symptoms. Is this person more nervous than usual? More angry or worried or distracted?

Now think about physical symptoms. Is this person complaining about headaches, stomachaches, back pain, and so on? Do these symptoms have a medical origin, or do you think they might be psychological?

Has this person started acting differently? Don't forget that behaving in a secretive manner could simply be a way to stake out some privacy or to get away from the pressures of the world. But it could also mean that the person is in fact keeping a secret. Is he or she spending more time alone, avoiding family or friends? Does this person attempt to explain away this remoteness or these absences with excuses that you have trouble believing?

Have you detected something different without knowing quite

how to put it into words? Do you have a gut feeling, an intuition about someone's private life, as if there's something on your radar that you can't quite identify but that you just somehow *know* doesn't match the public persona?

If the answer to more than one of these questions is yes, or if these concerns pretty much match your suspicions, then this person may be living a secret life. Now what? How do you handle the situation?

• **Approach, don't confront.** This is perhaps the most important distinction you can make in this kind of situation. If you confront the person, you can be sure that the wide, high, thick wall will remain impenetrable. Secret-keepers are already defensive. They're already, by definition, hiding something. If they sense they're being confronted, which can feel the same as being cornered, they might deny they're hiding anything and withdraw even further. They might even lash back, trying to turn the situation around, changing the subject by challenging you. "Oh, yeah? Well, you're no picnic to live with, either." "You want to know something that's been bothering me about you?" Or, worse: "Leave me alone," followed by a full emotional shutdown. So how do you approach secret-keepers without putting them on the defensive?

• **Use "I" instead of "you."** Don't say, "You're acting differently," or, "You're not there for me." Say, "I feel like you might be acting differently," "I sometimes feel that you're not 100 percent there for me," "I feel I miss you," "I feel like it's hard to reach you." And then follow up with, "What do you feel? What's your experience of this situation? Does what I'm feeling make sense to you?" Remember, the goal in approaching secret-keepers is not to catch them in an inconsistency or outright lie. It's not to make them feel ashamed or guilty. They're probably already feeling shame or guilt, and making them feel worse about themselves is only going to make the situation worse. Instead, the goal is to change the situation, perhaps even salvage a relationship.

• **Let them know you want to help.** You're on their side—and they need to hear this from you. Try to get them to understand that while, yes, only they can know what the secret they're harboring is, the *fact* of the secret is not a secret. Tell them that you've noticed changes in their behavior or their moods. Tell them that you can see the effect the secret life is having on them, and that you can see how those changes are having an effect on the way they relate to the outside world, including you. And don't hesitate to accept your share of the responsibility. Own up to it. Lead by example. If you've been an enabler—going out drinking with the secret alcoholic, or looking the other way when your partner comes home late twice a week—then say so. You'll be doing both of you a big favor.

• **Let them know that you want to help yourself, too.** Their secret life may be destroying your relationship, and while you want to ease their suffering, you also want to ease your own. You can and should let them know that you're angry or hurt. Make sure you express yourself in a nonpunitive way. The fact is, you're not concerned only about *their* well-being, and you shouldn't pretend you are. You're concerned about yourself, and you're concerned about your relationship with them, whatever it might be—as friends, family, lovers. By raising their awareness of how they're behaving and by explaining how that behavior is affecting you, you're providing a powerful motivation for them to get help. This puts you in a perfect position to take the next—and, with a little luck, the final—step:

- **Help them get help.** Whether "help" means hashing out the truth between yourselves in the privacy of your own home or whether it means seeing a professional, either individually or together, depends on the situation. As I mentioned in the previous chapter, sometimes professional help is the only realistic option. Some problems are simply too big for one person to overcome, even with the support of a dedicated friend or a community of friends and family. Whatever the individual case, if you're trying to get someone with an unhealthy secret life to examine the need for secrecy, then you have to be ready to help them not only sit and think about what they've done and why they've done it, but also act. It's not enough to answer the question, "What's wrong here?" The problem will linger and most likely resurface if you don't also answer the question, "Why?"

Now, a caveat. As the old saying (sort of) goes, "You can lead a horse to water, but you can't make him think." You might get the secret-keeper to admit to leading a secret life, and you might even get the secret-keeper to begin to examine why that secret life has taken root. But people change only when they want to. And they tend to want to change only when they *need* to. The needs of the secret-keeper in your life may not be the same as your own. You may have presented the most compelling case possible in terms of how their behavior is destroying their lives and hurting you. You may have pointed out that if they don't surrender their secret life they'll lose everything they love. Even so, they may not be able to change. The secret may have taken on a life of its own for psychological reasons even more compelling—that is, more satisfying, even if in some unhealthy way—than any argument you might make.

At that point, you may just have to walk away. That option might be the healthiest for you. If you have done everything in your power to help someone who is leading a secret life and they absolutely refuse to change, staying in that person's life will only lead to more lies and disappointment. But if the secret-keeper is willing to do the hard work of figuring out what the secret is and how it got there, then you might want to use, or suggest that the secret-keeper use, the following section as a guide.

IF YOU'RE LIVING A SECRET LIFE

You may already know that you're living a secret life. You're having an affair; you're a cocaine addict; you're a shoplifter. Or perhaps you merely suspect that you're living a secret life, but you don't know for sure. Either way, I want to offer some thoughts about how to approach your secret life.

Just as there are signs that others in your life might be leading secret lives, there are clues that suggest you might be hiding a secret life from yourself. Some of them might apply to you even if you're not leading a secret life, but these clues will give you plenty to consider.

Are you experiencing unusual or extreme emotions? Do you feel anxious or sad for reasons you can't identify? What about angry? Do you feel that you've removed yourself somehow from the familiar world around you, the world of family and friends? Have you found yourself obsessively repeating uncharacteristic nervous habits, such as biting your nails or drinking or smoking?

How do you feel physically overall? Exhausted? Do you have pains that defy medical explanation—headaches, stomachaches, back pain, and so on? Or maybe you've simply read something in this book that vaguely, disturbingly reminds you of you.

If these behaviors or patterns sound familiar and you either suspect or know that you're living a secret life, then I hope you'll want to ask yourself two essential questions. What is the source of the secret—what is the conflict that you hide from yourself, without even knowing it? And how can you overcome that secret? Here are a few suggestions to help you find the answers.

How do I find out where my secret life came from?

1. **Sit, don't act.** Living a secret life means acting out. It means that your fantasies have blurred into reality. Instead of thinking about having an affair, for example, you've actually begun having it. You've

taken action. If you're going to find out the meaning of your behavior, if you want to figure out why you're behaving the way you are, then you need to sit and think. Instead of behaving in a certain way, you need to ask yourself *why* you're behaving in a certain way. Somewhere in your past is the source of the conflict that compels you to act the way you do. What is it?

You need to clear some time for yourself. Find a point in your busy schedule when you can actually carve out some quiet and privacy. Turn off the TV, turn off the phone, send the kids out, close the door—do whatever it is that you need to do in order to get some quality time for yourself. And then *think*.

About what? Start with those secretive actions of yours. What is your secret life? What behaviors are actually involved? Where do you find yourself "screwing up" or acting in a manner that's destructive? Make a list. Try to identify the places where you find you're being the most destructive. The situations that give you the most anxiety. Which arena is it in? Family? Friends? Work? Love?

In a way, you're trying to "catch yourself in the act." You've probably seen a movie or TV cop look at a videotape from a security camera and suddenly yell, "Freeze it! Okay, now can you back it up a bit? Good. Now slow it down. Slower. And right . . . *there*!" That's sort of what I'm suggesting you do here. Find the scene in your life that seems to be the source of your anguish. Review the scene. Slow it down. And then try to zero in on the key piece of evidence.

Be specific about what you see on the "tape." Be honest. Be ruthless, in fact. Don't settle for anything less than the truth about yourself and your actions. Secret-keepers spend a lot of time justifying their actions. Try to look beyond the justification and denials. Ask yourself what it is that compels you to lead your secret life. What leads up to your secret-keeping? What circumstances tend to make you want to do things that must be hidden?

You'll want to flinch. Almost automatically, without even realizing it, you'll try to look away. Why? Because the behaviors you're witnessing have had an effect on your life, and they've probably had an effect on the lives of those close to you and might be a little bit horrified at what you're watching yourself do. You might feel ashamed or guilty. That would be a perfectly appropriate response. Just don't have it now. Instead:

2. Begin an anatomy of your secret life. Now is not the time to berate yourself. After all, your goal is not to cause yourself suffering. You're already suffering enough anyway—in ways you very likely don't even know. If you start to criticize yourself, chances are you're only going to shut down any further investigations and eliminate the chance for any further insights.

Instead, your goal right now is to observe the situation, because your goal overall is to *change* the situation. Ask yourself, what is your behavior? Where are you likely to engage in it? Do certain situations seem to exacerbate it? What effect does it have on you? What effect does it have on others?

And that's it. That's all you need to know at this point. Not: Are you a good person? Not: What kind of monster could possibly have done this?

Just: What are you doing?

3. Recognize you are not a victim. As you answer all these questions, you might very well feel powerless. You might feel as if you're watching someone else being caught in the act on the "videotape," as if that can't really be you, or if it is you, you must have been hypnotized, or sleepwalking. I can almost hear your protests, because I've often heard them from the patients in my own practice: "But it's not my fault, Dr. Saltz! It's not a choice!"

I agree, to a great extent. If you're living a secret life, then you probably have good reason to feel as if you have no control over it. In fact, you will probably feel as if the secret is controlling you. You'll feel as if this addiction is happening to you, this urge to shoplift is happening to you, this need to flirt with your husband's best friend is happening to you. And that's all true, because you are in fact at the mercy of the addiction, the urge, the need. These compulsions are out of your control. So I'll tell you what I tell my patients: You have a valid point. Something has happened to you that has rendered you pretty much powerless in this one area of your life. But I'll also tell you something else I tell my patients: You're still in charge.

Yes, the conflict at the heart of the secret has been controlling you, forcing you into psychological contortions that have basically led you to cut off a part of yourself and adopt a parallel, secret identity. But you're not just a passive victim. You are not the child to whom something happened twenty or thirty or forty years ago. You are no longer the child to whom a parent or teacher or sibling did something that created a conflict that in turn became the seed of the secret life you lead today. You are not a powerless child anymore.

You are a capable adult. You control your future. You are in charge of finding out what the conflict at the heart of your secret life is. You—and only you—can decide whether to uncover that conflict, and then to overcome it.

How do I overcome my secret?

1. Tell yourself the story of your secret. So far you have sat and thought about what your secret life is, looked at your behavior without passing judgment, and tried to shift from feeling like a powerless victim of your impulses to feeling like the person in charge of figuring out what's behind those impulses. Now it's time to ask yourself not only what the secret is but why it's important to you.

Why do you need to have that secret? Why do you need to keep that secret? In short, what do you imagine the benefits are?

Notice that I'm not asking, "What are the benefits?" I'm asking, "What do you *imagine* the benefits are?" That difference is crucial. It speaks to the core of the importance of the secret. You are hanging on to your secret life for dear life—literally. You feel that your very existence depends on doing whatever it is you do in secret. And you feel that if you stop doing it, you'll lose something you can't get anywhere else.

But what is that something? While leading your secret life, do you feel more satisfied, powerful, or calm? What feeling do you get while leading your secret life that keeps you coming back? Again, be precise, be truthful, be ruthless.

When you think you've found the answer, then try this:

2. Tell yourself the real story of your secret. This is the reality-check version of the story. Usually the story you tell yourself about why you live your secret life is a story that imagines the benefits. The reality-check version of the story, however, is the one that confronts the costs.

How is your secret life affecting your work, your relationships, and so on? If you have a secret drug habit, is it affecting your ability to perform sexually or to show up at work on time? If you have a secret affair, is it affecting the partner who thinks you're monogamous, or your relationship with your children? If the answer to this sort of question is yes, then you need to weigh these costs against the imagined benefits. For instance, is the high of the coke habit worth the loss of your job?

Of course, even if you recognize that the real-life costs far outweigh the imagined benefits, you still might not be able to change the secret life. The secret life holds a tremendous psychological power over you that has little to do with intellectual reasoning. Just because you know you might be hurting yourself doesn't mean you can will yourself to stop. So try this:

3. Tell yourself your other options. How might you live your life differently? Can you imagine a life without a secret life? How do you think it might feel? How do you think you might benefit? How do you think the people around you would benefit? What would you have to change? Think about Scott from earlier in the book. Suppose he'd spent his evenings getting work done or meeting with clients, rather than hiring escorts. Could that have helped his career?

4. Act, don't sit. When we started this discussion of what to do if you're living a secret life, I suggested that you *not* do what you always do in living a secret life, which is act on your impulses. Instead, I suggested that you sit and think. Now the time has come to reverse that process. Now you can turn the answer to the question *What would you have to change?* into action.

The first step might be a baby step. That's fine. That's progress. Even a baby step is a big step. Just as long as you do *something*, because all the thinking in the world is useless if it's not converted into action. Maybe you can confess the secret to someone (but be sure to choose a confidant who won't betray you). Or break off that secret relationship. If you don't want to tell someone you know about your addiction, tell someone you don't know: Go to an AA meeting. If you don't want to come out of the closet to the world at large, try coming out to your parents, or your sister, or a friend who won't be threatened.

But sometimes even a baby step is more than one person can

take without support. An inner conflict so pronounced, so profound, that it has led to the creation of a whole secret life is going to be difficult to find, let alone understand and reconceive. Seeing on the other side of the wall may well be impossible without someone else giving you a boost up. In that case, don't hesitate to seek professional help. It may be all that stands between you and a more satisfying life.

And that's the goal here: to lead that one life. Not a double life, not a parallel life, not a secret life. One life, examined, indivisible, whole.

[Appendix A]

Some Signs Someone You Know Is Living a Secret Life

You can't always be sure if someone you know is living a secret life or not, but people who have something to hide often exhibit some of the characteristics listed below.

- Seeming moody
- Acting nervous
- Exhibiting hair-trigger temper over small things
- Seeming beleaguered for no reason
- Seeming preoccupied and distant when you're with them
- Acting in suspicious ways, secretive ways, deceptively

- Spending unaccounted-for time on the phone, in the bathroom, or away from family and friends
- Responding "It's nothing" if asked about out-of-character behavior
- Behaving erratically
- Being unable to explain bills or missing money

[Appendix B]

Signs You're Hiding a Secret Life from Yourself

At this moment, you may not even realize you're hiding a secret life from yourself. Perhaps something is going on that is just too shameful for you to admit to yourself and you keep pushing it away. Look for some of these behaviors as signs that you may be keeping a secret from yourself:

- Feeling increasingly anxious for reasons you can't identify
- Feeling depressed or sad for reasons you can't identify
- Having angry outbursts or sudden bursts of rage over insignificant things

- Repeating a behavior, such as nail biting, drinking, or smoking, over and over again
- Feeling exhausted for no reason
- Experiencing physical ailments with no medical explanation—headache, stomachache, back pain, intestinal trouble

[Bibliography]

Bentley, Toni. *The Surrender*. New York: HarperCollins Publishers, 2004.

Carey, Benedict. "The Secret Lives of Just About Everybody." *New York Times*, January 11, 2005.

Cheever, Susan. *My Name Is Bill: Bill Wilson: His Life and the Creation of Alcoholics Anonymous*. New York: Simon & Schuster, 2004.

Freud, Sigmund. *The Standard Edition of the Complete Psychological Works of Sigmund Freud*. Translated under the general editorship of James Strachey, in collaboration with Anna Freud, assisted by Alix Strachey and Alan Tyson. London: The Hogarth Press and the Institute of Psycho-Analysis, 1953–66.

Fromkin, David. "The Importance of T. E. Lawrence." *The New Criterion*, September 1991.

Grafman, J., K. Schwab, D. Warden, A. Pridgen, H. R. Brown, and A. M.

Salazar. "Frontal Lobe Injuries, Violence, and Aggression: A Report of the Vietnam Head Injury Study." *Neurology* (1996), 1231–38.

Gross, Alfred. "The Secret." *Bulletin of the Menninger Clinic* (1951), 37–44.

Herek, Gregory J. "Gay People and Government Security Clearances: A Social Science Perspective." *American Psychologist* (1990), 1035–42.

Jacobs, Theodore J. "Secrets, Alliances, and Family Fictions: Some Psychoanalytic Observations." *Journal of the American Psychoanalytic Association* (1980), 21–42.

Kaplan, Louise. *Female Perversions: The Temptations of Emma Bovary.* New York: Doubleday, 1992.

Kelly, Anita E., and Kevin J. McKillop. "Consequences of Revealing Personal Secrets." *Psychological Bulletin* (1996), 450–65.

Kernberg, Otto F. "Sadomasochism, Sexual Excitement, and Perversion." *Journal of the American Psychoanalytic Association* (1991), 333–62.

Landler, Mark. "A Newspaper Reports Lindbergh Fathered 3 Children in Germany." *New York Times,* August 2, 2003.

Lane, Julie D., and Daniel M. Wegner. "The Cognitive Consequences of Secrecy." *Journal of Personality and Social Psychology* (1995), 237–53.

LaPeter, Leonora. "Some 70 Years After the Quiet Start of Alcoholics Anonymous, Its Basic Formula Is Applied Generously, with a Few Twists." *St. Petersburg Times,* March 15, 2004.

Last, Uriel, and Ahuva Aharoni-Etzioni. "Secrets and Reasons for Secrecy Among School-Aged Children: Developmental Trends and Gender Differences." *Journal of Genetic Psychology* (1995), 191–203.

Lawrence, T. E. *Seven Pillars of Wisdom: A Triumph*. Garden City, N.Y.: Doubleday, 1938.

"Lawrence, T. E." *Encyclopedia Britannica*. Encyclopedia Britannica Online. http://search.eb.com/eb/article-9047425.

"Lindbergh, Charles A." *Encyclopedia Britannica*. Encyclopedia Britannica Online. http://search.eb.com/eb/article-9048352.

"Lindbergh's Double Life," DW-World.de. http://www.dwworld.de/dw/article/0,1564, 1620936_0,00.html.

Margolis, Gerald J. "Secrecy and Identity." *International Journal of Psychoanalysis* (1966), 517–22.

———. "The Psychology of Keeping Secrets." *International Review of Psychoanalysis* (1974), 291–96.

Meares, Russell, and Wendy Orlay. "On Self-boundary: A Study of the Development of the Concept of Secrecy." *British Journal of Medical Psychology* (1988), 305–16.

Nabokov, Vladimir Vladimirovitch. *Lolita*. New York: Alfred A. Knopf, 1992.

"NIDA [National Institute on Drug Abuse] InfoFacts: Science-Based Facts on Drug Abuse and Addiction." http://www.nida.nih.gov/Infofacts/.

Norton, Rictor. "Gay Love-Letters from Tchaikovsky to His Nephew

Bob Davidof." *The Great Queens of History.* http://www.infopt.demon.co.uk/tchaikov.htm.

Ornstein, Anna, Cheryl Gropper, and Janice Z. Bogner. "Shoplifting." *Annual of Psychoanalysis* (1983), 311–31.

Pickert, Kate. "Stepdaddy's Little Girl." *New York,* April 11, 2005.

Ragins, Belle Rose, and John M. Cornwell. "Pink Triangles: Antecedents and Consequences of Perceived Workplace Discrimination Against Gay and Lesbian Employees." *Journal of Applied Psychology* (2001), 1244–61.

"Researchers Shed Light on Gambling and the Brain." http://www.sciencedaily.com/releases/2001/05/010524062100.htm.

Sulzberger, Carl Fulton. "Why It Is Hard to Keep Secrets." *Psychoanalysis* (1953), 37–43.

"Tchaikovsky, Pyotr Ilyich." *Encyclopedia Britannica*. Encyclopedia Britannica Online. http://search.eb.com/eb/article-9071483.

"Weekend Solo Hero." *Irish Times*, October 24, 1998.

Wegner, Daniel M., Julie D. Lane, and Sara Dimitri. "The Allure of Secret Relationships." *Journal of Personality and Social Psychology* (1994), 287–300.

Woolcott, Philip Jr. "Addiction: Clinical and Theoretical Considerations." *Annual of Psychoanalysis* (1981), 189–204.

[Index]

[About the Author]

© Sigrid Estrada

Dr. Gail Saltz is clinical professor of psychiatry at the New York Presbyterian Hospital Weill-Cornell School of Medicine. She is a psychoanalyst with the New York Psychoanalytic Institute and has a private practice on the upper east side of Manhattan. Dr. Saltz currently appears as a regular contributor on NBC's *Today* show. She was a weekly mental health contributor for ABC and Lifetime's show called *Lifetime Live,* is a frequent contributor to the A&E biography programs, and currently has a weekly relationship column on MSNBC.com.

Dr. Saltz has a series at the 92nd Street Y, where she interviews accomplished people in their field about psychologically interesting issues. She has interviewed Woody Allen, Tom Brokaw, Gail Sheehy, and Rosie O'Donnell. She is the author of *Becoming Real* and *5 Emotional Secrets to a Woman's Sexual Satisfaction.*

Visit Dr. Saltz at www.drgailsaltz.com.